47

ROSES

Also by Peter Sheridan

44: Dublin Made Me

47
ROSES

PETER SHERIDAN

VIKING

VIKING
Published by the Penguin Group
Penguin Putnam Inc., 375 Hudson Street,
New York, New York 10014, U.S.A.
Penguin Books Ltd, 80 Strand,
London WC2R 0RL, England
Penguin Books Australia Ltd, 250 Camberwell Road, Camberwell,
Victoria 3124, Australia
Penguin Books Canada Ltd, 10 Alcorn Avenue,
Toronto, Ontario, Canada M4V 3B2
Penguin Books India (P) Ltd, 11 Community Centre, Panchsheel Park,
New Delhi – 110 017, India
Penguin Books (N.Z.) Ltd, Cnr Rosedale and Airborne Roads, Albany,
Auckland, New Zealand
Penguin Books (South Africa) (Pty) Ltd, 24 Sturdee Avenue,
Rosebank, Johannesburg 2196, South Africa

Penguin Books Ltd, Registered Offices:
Harmondsworth, Middlesex, England

First American edition
Published in 2002 by Viking Penguin,
a member of Penguin Putnam Inc.

1   3   5   7   9   10   8   6   4   2

Excerpt from "When I'm Cleaning Windows," words by Harry Gifford and Fred E. Cliffe,
music by George Formby. Reprinted by permission of EMI Music Publishing Ltd.

LIBRARY OF CONGRESS CATALOGING-IN-PUBLICATION DATA
Sheridan, Peter, 1952–
47 roses / Peter Sheridan.
p.   cm.
ISBN 0-670-03100-3 (alk. paper)
1. Sheridan, Peter, 1952—Family. 2. Married people—Ireland—Dublin—Biography.
3. Triangles (Interpersonal relations)—Ireland. 4. Dramatists, Irish—20th century—
Biography. 5. Mothers and sons—Ireland—Dublin. 6. Dublin (Ireland)—Biography.
I. Title.

PR6069.H4575 Z465 2002
822'.914—dc21
[B]
2001057470

This book is printed on acid-free paper. ∞

Printed in the United States of America
Set in Weiss
Designed by Jaye Zimet

To the memory of my mother and father

Acknowledgments

This book would have been impossible without the support and encouragement of a great many people. My parents, Peter and Anna, inspired me all my life and they have not forgotten me since they departed this life.

I owe Sheila so much I wouldn't know where to begin, but her love and encouragement are the twin pillars of my life. My children, Rossa, Fiachra, Doireann and Nuala are my fiercest and most loyal critics. I bless them for their love. Viko, who has recently joined our family, is no less fierce and just as loyal.

Each of my wonderful family, Shea, Ita, Johnny, Frankie, Gerard and Paul, is a continuing source of inspiration to me. I cannot thank them sufficiently for their support and their openness.

My thanks to Pat Moylan, whose professional advice and friendship I couldn't do without. Also to her assistant, Emer Dooley, for her countless acts of kindness. Lucy McKeever, thank you for the litany of the saints. You will be canonized yourself some day.

My thanks to Beena Kamlani for her wonderful eye and attention to detail.

I am indebted to all the staff at Penguin who have helped bring this book to fruition. Darley Anderson, my agent, and his assistant, Kerith Briggs, thank you for your support and expertise.

Finally, thanks to Bill and Bob for everything they've done for me.

47

ROSES

Prologue

From as far back as I can remember, Da lied about his height. He claimed he was five foot six and a half with his shoes on, but he didn't look a centimeter over five foot four. At a push, he admitted to five foot five and a half, in his socks.

I suspected the lie from the time I was a kid. It was only when I grew up that I found him out for sure. I'm taller than Da, but I am only five foot five and a half, in my bare feet, independently measured, no bullshit. The horrible thing is that when I'm asked my height I always round it up to five foot six. Why do I need to be that extra half-inch taller? Why can't I be happy with what I am? Why do I have to inherit my father's complex? Do all men lie about their height because they believe it's a measure of their penis size?

Whatever the source of the complex, I inherited it, and when I was nineteen years old I fell in love with and married a woman who was three inches taller than me. For years I denied that the height differential threatened my masculinity. It was just that I always walked on the inside of the path because the ground was higher there. I convinced my wife, Sheila, to wear flat shoes for health reasons. I grew my hair long, did stretching exercises, and wore boots with heels because I was totally comfortable being small. Goddamn it, I wanted to be six feet tall. I grew up in a family where my sister, Ita, was four foot eleven and Ma was five foot one. That was the height I expected a woman to be. It wasn't in the script to fall in love with a woman who was five foot eight. As if that wasn't bad enough, Ma's first comment on meeting Sheila was that I'd have to grow a few inches to measure up. Having been nailed to the cross by my forebears, living and dead, I soldiered on in denial for many years.

The issue of height started in our house at an early age. On our second birthdays, after the candles were blown out, Da ceremoniously measured each one of us. I stood against the inside of the kitchen door and felt the ruler on the top of my head. Where the ruler hit the door was marked with a lead pencil, and beside it my name in block capitals. Shea had a mark, Ita had a mark, then there was me, and later Johnny. Da told me I would be twice that height when I was a fully grown man. He measured it up the door, and it came out at five foot five and a half. It seemed high in the sky when I was two looking up. Bit by bit, I made strides towards the mark. I would stand under it every so often and see how much more I had to go. Sometimes I did it every day, to see could I catch myself growing. One time, I grew two inches in a day. I was so excited I thought I was going to be a giant. I brought everyone over to the door and showed them. Johnny pointed out that the other mark was his. Everyone started to call me "midget." In the middle of the dinner, someone would look at me and whisper the word. Then everyone would fall about except Ma and Da.

I had to find ways to measure myself in secret. When I came

in from school or a football match, I'd close the door behind me and pretend I was taking off my coat. I'd lean back against the door, put my hand on my head, and step out to see was there any change from the day before. I could do it in a matter of seconds with not the slightest chance of being caught.

By the time Ita was twelve, she'd reached her adult mark on the kitchen door. She stood with her back against it and her head came up to the pencil mark put there by Da ten years earlier. She was inconsolable. The tears were streaming down her face and she couldn't stop them. Ma was trying to console her, and Ita was talking ten to the dozen, but it was very hard to make out her words through the sobs. She was only twelve and her life was over. It was the saddest thing in the world to see Ita upset, because there was nothing you could do about your height. It was your mother's and father's fault, it was a genetic thing, and they were to blame. Ma didn't see it that way. She blamed Da for causing all the trouble with his nonsense on the back door. Ma took charge. She boiled up a kettle of water and poured it into a basin. She got out her best worst cloth, the one for heavy stains, which had been a pair of Da's trousers once, and she approached the door like a matador entering the ring. She stared the pencil marks straight in the eye. From left to right, Shea, Ita, Peter, Johnny, Frankie, Gerard, and Paul.

— Bastards, your days are done.

The shouts went up around the house. It was a universal cry of protest. We pleaded and begged Ma, we cursed her and we prayed for her, we implored and we beseeched her, Mother of God, not to do the dastardly deed. Shea and I got between Ma and the door. Frankie and Johnny grabbed her by the arms, one apiece, and tried to pull her back. Gerard and Paul looked on at their first family fight. It was no use, Ma was determined, and when Ma was determined no human force could stop her. She was about to wipe out our history, the nearest thing we had to a family tree. The marks on the door were who we were, and they were about to face the firing squad, and no Da to save them.

Ma carried the basin and dragged Frankie and Johnny in her wake towards the door. Shea threatened to spill the hot water on the floor. I threatened I'd go to the train station and get Da. Ma was fearless in the face of these threats. Da said once it was a pity you couldn't plug Ma in because she'd light every room in the house. He was wrong, of course: she'd light every room in Seville Place, and the street lamps, too. She stood before us, all five foot one of her, and she held up the suds-soaked cloth.

— Troublemakers, that's all yous are.

Ma was addressing the pencil marks. It was something she often did, personalizing inanimate objects, she did it so she could attack them better. It helped her stir up her emotions and gave her strength. Shea and I tried to shield as much of the door as we could. Ma bobbed and weaved in front of us until she caught sight of Ita's mark. She landed a perfect right cross, bang in the center of the target. As she pummeled it to oblivion, Ita sprang up like a phoenix from her chair, begging Ma to stop. It took a couple of seconds for Ita's plea to register, and by the time it dawned on Ma, we were all screaming at her to stop, Ita loudest of all. When Ma withdrew her hand, the adult mark was gone. Ita was hysterical. Five minutes after the attack on the door had begun, Ita was standing with her back to it once more and Ma was making her four-foot-eleven mark with the aid of Da's lead pencil. Ita was restored to her place on the kitchen door, and the family was intact once again.

1

It was a typical January Friday at the bus station in Dublin—cold, gray, and chaotic. Nowhere on earth breeds confusion like the Irish transport system. The "bus depot," its name in English, is also known as Busáras, its name in Gaelic. Every bus has two destinations, so that if you're traveling to Dundalk it's vital to know that it's also called Dún Dealgan. To add to the mayhem, some buses depart from inside the perimeter of the station and some depart from out on the road. No one is ever there to tell you, because it is a state secret. When you do find your bus, you can be certain the door will be closed and a crowd of forlorn people will have formed themselves into a queue.

I was heading to Derry, also known as Londonderry, where I was to conduct a weekend workshop on a play entitled *William and Mary*. It had been sent to me by a young Derry writer, Malachy Martin, whom I'd met at a writers' conference in Belfast. The protagonist of the piece was the Dutchman William of Orange, a hate figure for so many Irish Catholics after his victory over James II at the Battle of the Boyne in 1690. I had been educated to hate William for the same reasons I'd been taught to hate Glasgow Rangers Football Club—they were blue, royalist, right-wing, bigoted, Protestant, and triumphalist.

My anti-William bias was soon confounded. For starters, he was an only child and had no one to play with. Because he was a prince, he wasn't allowed to mix. Those around him were very concerned about his schooling and his strict religious education, but they couldn't see that he needed friends more than anything else in his life. He needed to go to the beach and learn to swim and go on messages for his father, like an ordinary child. Unfortunately, his father died while William was still in his mother's womb. As if he weren't misfortunate enough, his mother died when he was eight years old and left him completely alone in the world. My brother Frankie died when he was ten, and it nearly ripped our family apart. At least I had four other brothers and a sister to help me get over it. William had no one, neither family nor friend, and he was left to grow up completely and utterly on his own.

He grew up to be five foot five and a half, but he had no complex about his height. He had his pick of any princess in Europe, including the dauphiness of France, but he married his first cousin, Mary, against all comers. She was six inches taller than he, a fact that would have intimidated most men. William used to boast about his wife's height, and in public they always walked hand in hand, like true lovers. The fashion of the day for men was pomandered wigs, but William refused to wear one and instead grew his own hair down to his bum, so that many of his contemporaries thought he looked like a woman. What they didn't know was that William, in private, dressed as a woman, too. How could I dislike this feminine, eccentric man with whom I shared such a vital statistic?

I was standing in the line to buy a bus ticket and thinking

about William's femininity when an image of Da came into my mind. I was four years old in my grandfather's house and everyone was laughing. Da came into the dining room, dressed as a woman, kicking his feet in the air doing the cancan. Aunties Anne, Lily, and Marie, Da's three sisters, were hysterical, and I was crying, but they told me to shush, that it was only Da dressed up. I tried to stop and was wiping my tears away when Uncle Paddy followed Da into the room dressed like him and trying to kick his legs in the air, but he was laughing so much that he nearly fell over. We poured out onto Friary Avenue, a little street at the back of the Capuchin friary where Granddad and Granny Sheridan lived, and I watched Da and Uncle Paddy arse their way down the avenue. I remembered Ma throwing her eyes to heaven and saying, "That's Da for you." All the kids chased after them as far as the pub, and we watched them at the counter ordering drinks like two aul' wans.

Da brought us into a special place called the snug that was full of gummy old women sipping balls of malt. He put six glasses and a large bottle of red lemonade on the table in front of us. When he poured it out, the froth came to the top and over the side, and we licked it off with our tongues and some went up my nose and I sneezed. I didn't mind Da being a woman if it meant red lemonade every day.

Da dressed as a woman because he loved showing off. Every day from nine until five he sold train tickets in Amiens Street Station. Three nights a week he calculated the payouts at the greyhound track in Shelbourne Park. There wasn't a lot of time for showing off in between, so when the opportunity presented itself he took it. That was mainly at Christmastime, and it became Da's season for dressing up. And Uncle Paddy's, too.

I was delighted to make a connection between William and Da, even though they dressed up for very different reasons. It felt like a link between the past and the present, and one that could be developed with the actors in the workshop. How many men would admit to having tried on women's underwear? How would the actors react if I told them they had to live as transvestites for a month? It was going to be a mischievous weekend. I couldn't wait to get there.

I purchased my ticket and found the Derry Express. Predictably, the door of the bus was closed, and a queue had formed. An elderly lady who looked like Popeye's partner, Olive Oyl, grabbed the sleeve of a gray-capped man who looked official. She wanted to know why the door of the bus was closed. He turned and listened to her in disbelief, then bent his face down close to hers. He pointed to his forehead.

— Informayshun. Do you see that written on my forehead? No, you don't, because I'm not informayshun. Go to the desk if you want informayshun.

Meanwhile, a man in a cream shirt and black baggy trousers approached our bus. He had on a company tie that made him look as if he were attempting suicide by strangulation. In one hand he carried a black metal box, and in the other he had a clipboard. A bunch of keys dangled from his belt, and a cigarette of gray ash protruded from his lips. I'd have taken odds his mother christened him Benjy. He opened up a panel in the side of the bus and started to fling suitcases into the bowels with abandon. He was good-humored and jolly and didn't seem to care that the crack at the top of his arse was open to public view. Benjy crawled in after one or two stubborn cases, thumped them lovingly with his fist, and backed out again. When he stood up and looked around, the ash on his cigarette was still intact. All my life I've wondered how some men do that.

Olive Oyl arrived back on the arm of a bus inspector and was escorted onto the bus ahead of everyone else. At that point, all decorum was abandoned. We hustled to get on the bus like bees trying to enter a hive. Ten would-be passengers failed to make it, and I tried not to look at their broken-hearted faces as they wandered aimlessly up and down the aisle, looking for seats that weren't there. Out on the tarmac, it looked like an eviction scene. A dispossessed husband and wife were waving bus tickets with the authority of tenants holding a fully paid up rent book. A bald gentleman with a serious beard, who looked like a visiting German poet, was quietly pleading in his native tongue that he had to board the bus. Back inside, Benjy of the cracked arse made an announcement.

— This bus terminates at Monaghan.

The explosion was immediate. People were on their feet shouting, and Benjy was telling them to keep their hair on. Irate passengers wanted to know why they weren't on the Derry Express.

— Passengers for Derry change at Monaghan. If you stay on this bus you'll end up back in Dublin, do yous get me?

Outside, the war of words was raging. Three hundred and five years after the first Siege of Derry, the Busáras stand-off was taking hold. Paralysis. Stasis. Immobility. A European dimension was brought by the German poet, who was standing in front of the bus. Benjy turned over the engine and revved it up to show he wasn't going to be intimidated. The German started to lose it when Benjy covered him in black smoke. He pulled at his beard in temper. Benjy put the bus in gear and eased it out of its bay. The German ran in front of the bus and Benjy slammed on the brakes. The inspector came in front, waving a white handkerchief of surrender. Benjy gushed open the air door and brought the stand-off to an end. The inspector boarded the bus, followed by the German, who turned out to be a Polish Catholic from Warsaw. He explained his origins by way of blessing himself hundreds of times and invoking the name of John Paul II. The Pole apologized for holding up our journey, performing an excellent mime that made it clear he had something in the hold, namely his bicycle. Benjy knew that enormous damage had been done to the tourist image of Ireland, and he broke every rule under the sun by offering the Pole a seat on the floor by the steps, which, after a minor protest, he accepted. Finally, the Derry Express, which wasn't an express and went to Monaghan, was on the road and heading in a northerly direction. I was delighted to be on the road at last, making a pilgrimage to the last remaining walled city in Europe. I closed my eyes and dreamt about Da and William. Had the young Dutchman been a lodger in our house (we'd had over forty through the years), Da would undoubtedly have challenged him to a wrestling match. I was imagining them locked together on the floor and Ma stepping over them to pour out the tea when the Derry Express hit a pothole that shot us from our seats. My briefcase toppled out of the overhead rack and hit me on the face. There were minor calamities throughout the bus while Benjy of the cracked arse switched on the intercom and made an announcement.

— This is pothole country; for your safety, please remain seated.

The bus pulled into a car park in Monaghan. We filed off into a canteen where a long queue had formed. They'd run out of sandwiches just before we arrived, and all available staff were now in the kitchen frantically putting butter on bread. I could hear the distinctive slap of cheese on bread from where I was standing. The sandwiches came out in a cortège to the counter, and there was a further delay while girls in white coats put them into plastic containers and recorded their contents and sell-by dates on a label down the side. It was torture on a Biblical scale. We waited in silence while King Benjy of the cracked arse unwrapped his homemade crispy bacon sandwiches and plunged his molars in. And still we waited.

After all the shenanigans with the sandwiches, it turned out they were all the same—plain cheese on white bread with butter. I tried to explain to the girl the silliness of putting them in containers when they were all the same. She was having none of it.

— Blame Europe, it's them ones make us do it.

I took my plastic container of bread and cheese along with all the other helpless sheep and I searched for somewhere to chew the cud. The only chair left was at Benjy's table. I sat opposite him, took the manna from its tabernacle, and stuffed it in my mouth. Benjy lit a cigarette and blew the smoke down my throat just as I swallowed the first mouthful. I went into a fit of coughing that brought the bread back up onto the plate.

— Awful fucking sandwiches, aren't they?—he said.

I tried to catch my breath and stop spluttering. He offered me a cigarette. I waved him away.

— No smoking here from next month—he said.— Soon we won't be able to piss. I blame Europe.

I recovered enough to speak. I confessed I'd quit smoking, in the vague hope that Benjy might take pity on me and put out his cigarette.

— I'd die if I had to quit smoking—he said.—Sure it's the only vice left now.

I looked at Benjy's angelic face, which was a perfect match for his arse. Two beautiful, pale orbs, the kind that inspired poetry.

— Who do you blame for the potholes?—I said.

Benjy's face lit up. He blew smoke down the twin pipes of his nose, leaned in close, and whispered conspiratorially.

— There wasn't a pothole in Ireland before we joined up with Europe.

I couldn't get my head around Benjy's logic. Every time I looked at him I saw a sign that read: *No exposed arses—by order from Europe*. When I finished my smoked-cheese sandwich, I said goodbye and headed out to find the bus that would take me to Derry.

We crossed the border at Aughnacloy and hit the smooth roads of Northern Ireland, where potholes are virtually unknown. We made our way along country roads past villages that had their curbstones painted in red, white, and blue for loyalty to the Crown, or green, white, and orange for loyalty to the Irish Republic. I could hear Lambeg drums echo in the sound of the tires on the road outside.

Derry revealed itself hunkered below us with Creggan Graveyard on the hill like a testament to the city's troubled past. As we swept down the hill and turned left to cross Craigavon Bridge, passengers stood up and pulled their bags from the overhead racks. We turned into the bus depot, and an inspector stood in front of the bus and brought it to a halt. He boarded and asked everyone to sit down.

— Is there a Mr. Sheridan aboard?—he asked.

I knew it couldn't be me. I looked around to see the passenger I shared a name with. No one responded. The inspector repeated his call. I felt awkward leaving him standing there when at least I had the right name. I put my hand up, but I knew he wasn't looking for me. He came down the aisle and asked me in a very quiet tone was my wife's name Sheila. I was completely taken aback.

— You've to ring home for an urgent message—he informed me.

I had that sinking feeling there was something the matter with one of the children. I had two sons, Rossa and Fiachra, studying in the United States. Could it be they'd had an accident? Or could it be Doireann or Nuala, my two daughters, who were at school and lived at home? My brother Frankie died in 1967, when I was fifteen. As I stepped off the bus, it was 1967 again. My mouth went dry. I felt utterly alone. Was it Nuala?

She was the baby, and the wildest. I prayed that she'd had a regular accident. I inserted the coins and for a moment I couldn't remember my phone number. I was thinking of an old number, long since defunct, when the current one came back to me. I pressed the digits with great care and waited for a reply. Doireann answered, and I knew there was something wrong.

— Hi, Doireann, it's Dad—I said.

When she heard my voice, she broke into tears, and she tried to get words out, but they choked in her sobs. Finally, she said "Granddad," and she just kept repeating it through the tears, one word, repeated, trying to find other words that wouldn't come, but all she could find was "Granddad."

— Granddad . . . Granddad . . . Granddad . . . —she sobbed.

— What's wrong with Granddad?—I asked.

I knew what was wrong with Granddad. I had imagined his death many times, but nothing prepares you for the moment.

— Granny found him at two o'clock, there was nothing she could do—she said.

— Where did Ma find him?—I asked.

— On the floor of the sitting room.

— Did he have a heart attack?

— I don't know. Granny called the ambulance, but it was no good. It wasn't her fault, Dad.—She started to get upset again.

— Of course it wasn't her fault. You stay where you are and mind Nuala. I'll see you later. Goodbye.

I replaced the receiver, and from the corner of my eye I saw Malachy Martin walk towards me. We shook hands and hugged like theatre people do. I didn't want to tell him about my father. If I told him, I would confirm it, and I wasn't ready yet. I knew it was true, but I didn't want to give it expression. What was I to do? If he was dead, why hadn't I felt his spirit tug at my sleeve for permission to go? Why had I not received a sign? I remembered the bus plunging into the pothole at two o'clock. Doireann had mentioned two o'clock on the phone as the time of his collapse.

I told Malachy something had come up and I might have to go home early. That was as far as I could go. I wouldn't disappoint the actors now that I was here. I'd inherited my father's work ethic, and I wouldn't let them down. I excused myself and went off to phone Ma. Soon as I heard her voice, the tears came, and I couldn't stop them. They spilled into the phone as I listened to her.

— Oh, Pete, Pete, I came back from the neighbor's and he was on the floor. If I'd been there I could have done something. He was marking the racing results when I left him, I thought he was OK, but I should have known. Oh, Pete, I should have been here.

— No, you shouldn't, Ma. It's not your fault. I'll be home tonight—I said. I walked over to Malachy and gave him the news.

— I have to go home and bury my father—I said.

Malachy walked me to the tarmac, and I boarded the lousy Derry Express that was bound for Dublin. I sat in the same lousy seat, closed my eyes, and willed it to be in Dublin. As the bus crossed the Foyle, I opened my eyes and I could see the pale reflection of the yellow street lights in the lousy river below. As the light disappeared from the sky, sleet started to fall out of the darkness. A big blob landed beside me on the window and clung to it like it wanted to get in. I closed my eyes. When I opened them again, it had fallen off.

2

Da was lying on a slab in a hospital morgue, but I couldn't picture him. It was completely out of character for him. He didn't lie still, ever. Never closed his eyes for rest. There was no morgue anywhere could contain Da's spirit. No doctor or mortician would convince Da to get up on a slab and play dead to the world.

I couldn't picture him. I wanted to picture him, because I didn't want him to be alone. Morgues were lonely, frightening places. I didn't want him on his own there. Not with other people who were dead and wanted to be on slabs. Da had never been on a winter holiday. He had never been skiing. He had never been to a place with packed snow and ice. All Da knew was warmth and summer swimming in the sea and being the first to take the plunge when the rest of us stood shivering on the rocks.

— What's it like, Da?
— Soup.

Only word he ever used to describe the sea. Soup. He warmed it up for us. You could see the excited bubbles ripple out from his hairy chest. Turned the sea into a heated swimming pool. All five foot four and a half of him. Splash, splash, splash, splash, splash. Shea, Ita, me, Johnny, and Frankie. Steps of watery stairs swimming in his slipstream. Loughshinny, Skerries, Rush, Bray, Greystones, and Brittas. Every beach north and south of the Liffey, every beach reachable by train from Amiens Street Station. We, the proud possessors of privilege tickets, which got us there for nothing because of Da's job.

Ma sat on the beach with the younger ones, Gerard and Paul, making hot tea for the returning swimmers. The mad rush up the beach to secure the best towels. Da declining all offers to dry himself.

— What was it like, Da?

— Soup.

He stood on the sand with his barrel-of-Guinness tummy pointing out to sea. He slapped the spare flesh on his back with great swinging arcs of his arms, like an ape up in the zoo. All around him the tribe of chattering teeth struggled to get their vests on.

— How can you not be freezing, Da?

— Because the sea is like soup.

Ma handed out the tea. The secret was not to drink it but to nestle it in your hands until the life came back into your fingers. After that you could press it against your face or hold it tight between your legs until your privates warmed up. Da didn't need to do any of that. His tea went straight into his mouth and washed his sandwich down. He sat in his wet togs and looked out to sea like it was home. The sea was his element, and it caressed him like it loved him. The salt, the surf, the seaweed all tingled when they saw him coming, and he was carefree and abandoned among them like nowhere else I knew.

The sea around Ireland would suffer with Da gone. He kept it warm, year in and year out. It was impossible to believe he was going cold, and I did believe it but only in a remote sort of way, in the same way I believed that Australia existed.

I'd forgotten to ask where they'd taken him. I was so angry with myself for forgetting to ask. Had I known where he was, I might have been able to picture him. As it was, I had to play mental charades.

I pictured myself walking up to the front door of every Dublin hospital I knew. Jervis Street, the Mater, the Richmond, the Meath, Sir Patrick Duns, St. Vincent's. I ignored reception and followed the signs for mortuary and found myself being taken there by a man with a glass eye and a twisted leg. He wore a turf-brown coat beloved of hospital porters. I was anxious to get to Da, but in order not to overtake this man, I had to walk at half my normal speed. It struck me more than once along the way that he had been given this job because his disfigurement prepared distraught relatives for what they were about to see, by reminding them of their own mortality.

When we got to the door of the mortuary, he took a bunch of keys from his pocket and held them up to the light. He examined the credentials of each key before he chose one to put in the lock. I followed him into this place of eerie silence. There were a number of slabs and bodies covered with sheets. It looked like a gallery and felt like a chapel. There were pillars at one end, and I could see a figure lurking behind them. It was Da. He stepped out and started to walk towards us. He had his Saturday work clothes on, and he was fiddling in the trouser pocket the way he would when he was fishing for money to send me on one of his messages. He told the porter he was slipping out for a cup of tea, and he offered him a fistful of money. The glass-eyed porter returned him an unbribable stare. Da held out the money, and I could see his hand was shaking with the cold. His lips and his ears were blue, and his temples were blue, and he was trying hard not to shake. I was glad to see him, of course I was, but it was pathetic seeing him trying to bribe his way out. I didn't want him doing this if he was meant to be on a slab. I wanted him to accept his situation, and I was angry that he wasn't laid out like an ordinary dead person.

It was arctic on the Derry Express. The sleet was still falling, and there was a numbing wind blowing up from underneath the seats, making icicles of my feet. It was little wonder that Da was running about the mortuary in my thoughts, blue with the cold and refusing to get under his sheet. I couldn't resist the feeling that it was an illusion and once I got home I'd be able to fix it and put things right. Da couldn't leave us just like that. It wasn't in his nature. It wasn't in our family tradition. We said goodbye before we departed this world. That's how it was with Frankie when he died, and that's how it was with Granddad Sheridan. It was sad, it was upsetting, but it was the right way.

I was ten years old when I was sent into Granddad's bedroom in Friary Avenue. He had asked to see all the grandchildren, and we went up the stairs and into the return room one by one. I had never been in a dying person's room before. The blind was drawn and the light was on, which gave the room a yellow tint. Granddad asked me how I was getting on at school. His voice was weak from all the cigarettes he had smoked, which gave him the cancer that had rotted his lungs. But I think he was still smoking. When I told him I got first place in the class exams, he coughed his guts up, which was a real giveaway. I decided I was never going to smoke. When Granddad stopped coughing, he asked me what Santy was bringing me for Christmas. It was a silly question. I was almost eleven and didn't believe in Santy. I didn't want to upset him, so I was thinking up an answer when he asked me to turn out the light. I flicked the switch and the room went dark. As soon as I did, Granddad sat up straight and called out in a strong voice that had no hint of a cough:

    — Father Albert, it's good to see you, come in—he said.

Father Albert was the Capuchin monk from Church Street who went down to the Four Courts in 1916 and told the men to get out just before the British started to shell it. Granddad was a quartermaster of the Four Courts Garrison, and Father Albert was a hero among the men. Years later, when Granddad and some of his IRA comrades went political and founded the Fianna Fáil Party, they called the very first branch Cumann Albert, after Father Albert.

    — I want to make a confession, Father.

How could I hear my grandfather's confession when I was only a ten-year-old boy?

    — I shot an informer. Out in the back stable. I didn't know he was married, Father—he said in a low voice.

    — I'm not Father Albert—I said.

    — Who are you?—he asked.

    — I'm Peter Martin, Granddad—I said.

Granddad beckoned me to sit on the bed, and I did. He repeated my name several times, until his breath ran out and my name lodged in his chest. For a minute I thought he was dead. He took my hand in his and squeezed a coin into it. I knew it was a half-crown by the size of it.

    — Don't forget your granddad, sure you won't?—he said.

I shook my head. I didn't know if he could see me in the confession-box darkness of the room.

    — I won't forget you, Granddad—I said.

He squeezed my hand again, and I was glad I'd said it out loud.

That Christmas was the first year Uncle Paddy and Da didn't dress up as women. They took Granddad and his bed down to the sitting room and lit the biggest fire I'd ever seen. Everyone was going around with the veins in their faces showing. Granddad perked up, and we all had to sing or do a recitation for him. Ita and I sang "The Black Hills of Dakota" as a duet. Johnny did a poem he'd learned in school.

> — Two little dickey birds sitting on a wall,
> One named Peter and one named Paul.
> Fly away Peter, fly away Paul.
> Come back Peter, come back Paul.

Da sang "Ol' Man River" in a deep voice and got everyone to join in on the chorus. By that stage it was a noble call, which meant that the last singer nominated the next person to sing. Da called on "Mother," who was my granny.

> — Order for the woman of the house.

Granny protested that she had no voice, but no one paid the slightest heed to her. She settled herself and wetted her whistle before launching into "Tri-Colored Ribbon O." Granny wasn't the greatest singer, but there was passion in her voice like she was pouring her heart out.

> — I had a true love, if ever a girl had one.
> I had a true love, a brave lad was he.
> One fine Easter Monday with his gallant comrades
> He started away for to make old Ireland free.

By the chorus, everyone should have been joining in, but there was one voice only in the room. One voice only in Friary Avenue. One voice only in Ireland. Everyone was holding back

the tears while Granny said goodbye to Granddad. We all knew
it was a final farewell.

> — *And if anybody asks me the reason why I'm wearing it*
> *It's all for my true love I never more will see.*

Two weeks to the day after Christmas, Granddad gave up
the fight. He was laid out in Friary Avenue, and the wake went
on for two days and two nights. His comrades came by to pay
their respects to an old soldier, a true Gael, and a fearless de-
fender of the Republic. I heard one of them say that Granddad
had lost faith in politics after "the long fellow," Éamon De
Valera, signed the oath of allegiance and went back into the
Dáil. When they took Granddad from the house to the church,
the priest said that life springs from death and that it is in dying
we are born again. I believed him, because Granddad had died
on my eleventh birthday, January 8, 1963. He could have left us
on Christmas night, after Granny's song, but he held on until
my birthday so that I would always carry the memory of him
with me into the future.

Nineteen sixty-three was a watershed, and Friary Avenue
was never the same again. The clan gathered the following
Christmas night, but it was a party without the host, a party
with sadness at its core. The adults made us sing and pretended
that Christmas was for young people.

> — It's all about the young fry.
> — What would Christmas be without the young fry?
> — We have to do it for the young fry.

But the young fry knew it was all about the adults and the
adults being children again. Christmas was Da and Uncle
Paddy dressing up as women and waddling down Friary Avenue
to the hollers of aunts and uncles, the delight of neighbors, the

amazement of strangers, and kids following at their heels, always kids following at their heels. After Granddad's death, they never dressed as women again. Within a few years, we stopped going to Friary Avenue altogether and the Christmas night party happened in our house, 44, and Da became the master of ceremonies. He got the entertainment going by dancing around the floor and balancing a bottle of Guinness on his head without spilling a drop. Whatever way the top of his head was made, it was perfect for balancing bottles, and no one ever came near him in the annual competition.

Now Christmas had changed forever again. Nineteen ninety-four would become another watershed. Six days after my birthday, and Da was gone. No farewells, no goodbyes, gone. No lung cancer, no disease, just dead. For someone so gregarious, it seemed preposterous. Three weeks earlier, he had entertained the grandchildren with the bottle trick. There was no sense of a departure. He had sung "Frankie and Johnny" with all his old gusto, performing the actions with the words right down to the dramatic finale, when Frankie shoots her man three times, rat-a-tat-tat. His noble call was me, and I sang George Formby's "Cleaning Windows." I'd sung it for him hundreds of times, and he still laughed at the saucy bits like he was hearing them for the first time.

— *Pajamas lying side by side,*
Ladies' nighties I have spied.
I've often seen what goes inside,
When I'm cleaning windows.

Sitting on the Derry Express as it sludged its way towards Dublin, I felt sad about Da, but I wanted to feel sadder, much sadder. I wanted to be physically there, I wanted to stand beside him and see him laid out on the slab, but he wouldn't lie down in my thoughts. I couldn't get it out of my brain that I owed him money and would never have the chance to pay him back.

As a young married student, I'd taken out a loan to buy a mobile home. I was determined to set up on my own with Sheila, and after a row with Da (he believed marriage would ruin my university career), we moved out to Crumlin and away from the inner city. It was a titanic struggle, and money was very scarce, even after graduation. What could I expect, choosing a career in the theatre. The letters from the bank went unopened into the bin, and when we moved back to the city, the letters dried up completely. That's how it stayed until, after a gap of two and a half years, a letter arrived in our door. In the top right-hand corner were written the words "Student Loan." I cursed the bastards and threw it in the bin. Then I had an idea, an insane idea, but I thought it might work. I would ask the bank to sponsor my writing. I would write a play and put their name above the title, and in return they would write off my student debts.

The bank manager was beaming. He took me into his office. We made small talk about the benefits of third-level education while he took out my file and spread it before him. It was seven years since I'd sat in this chair and lied about wanting to be a secondary-school teacher. A nice, respectable, hardworking, salaried, dependable schoolteacher.

— The repayments you made were consistent. That's good.

— What repayments?

— The ones you made to pay off the loan.

I looked at this man in a suit and realized I was about to become the beneficiary of a great banking error. I had come to seek out a sponsorship deal and, inadvertently, I'd gotten it.

The Bank of Ireland presents, through no fault of its own, *The Student Loan* by Peter Sheridan. I stroked my nose with my fingers, long, languorous strokes. I slid them down onto my lips and pulled at the flabby bits. It was to stop me from opening my mouth and talking. At the end of the interview, the bank manager offered me further loan facilities, if and when I needed them. I refused everything in order to get out of there and celebrate. Momentarily, I ran out of the university branch of the Bank of Ireland and roared all the way down to the Stillorgan Road, where I hailed a taxi. I couldn't wait to give Sheila the news.

Crossing Butt Bridge, there was a monstrous traffic jam, and we crawled bumper to bumper around Beresford Place and onto Amiens Street. In the distance was the train station, standing sentry as always, facing Talbot Street and the city to the west and behind it Seville Place and Sheriff Street to its east. It shielded my childhood and looked out on my adult world. Da had worn out its granite steps for thirty years now. Day in and day out, up and down to the ticket office, he knew every grain and blemish in its character. I no sooner had the thought than I saw him coming out of Terry Rogers Bookies, opposite the station. He had his newspaper stuffed in the side pocket of his brown suit, open on the racing page. I rolled down the window to call him, and nothing came out of my mouth. It was as if an instinct far deeper than thought had paralyzed me. In that moment, I realized that it was the granite steps had paid my student loan. I looked at his squat figure, just under five foot six, I looked at his shape and the Dublin walk of him, the way he leaned on his shoes so that they forever needed leather surgery on one side, the shoulders back, and the swinging arms that made him proud but without the sin of pride, the blocky head with the inquisitive face open to the world, and the forehead that swelled under the weight of ideas and the pain of stored secrets. He had paid my loan without telling me. I watched him go up the granite steps and felt chastened and humbled by his sacrifice. I swore that one day I would pay him back. One day.

The thought that I could never repay him was painful beyond words. Settling my account with Da would have told him, in our secret way, that I'd succeeded in the real world. The fact that I would never have that opportunity was a pain in my gut like I'd never had before. Why did you have to die, Da, could you not have waited?

The bus stopped at the Monaghan hitching post, but I stayed in my seat. I was thinking about his secrets. What was he taking to his grave with him? It seemed surreal that he was lying on a slab in a place unknown, lying silent. I was rushing back to be with him, to ask him the questions I needed to ask him before he was gone forever. It was illogical, but I felt if I was there he'd be all right somehow. Once I got home, things would be OK.

I wondered had he ever told Ma about my student loan. I could picture him at the table writing in his ledgers. He recorded every transaction he made with the world. Every wages slip had its own entry. All expenditure was spelt out in his neat, decisive handwriting. It was like he'd made a pact with God to keep an inventory of his life in the form of an income/expenditure account. His good and bad deeds could be read there, by those who had the key. House insurance, including liability for lodgers and guests, five shillings and sixpence. Student loan for A. N. Other, eight shillings a month. Contribution to church restoration, two shillings and sixpence. Investment with bookies (loss), twelve pounds even. Investment with bookies (profit), see previous entry. Good-luck donation to St. Anthony, half-crown. Switch to St. Jude, patron saint of hopeless cases, for the coming year. Christmas gift for Doris, including post and package, six shillings and sixpence. Petrol for car, nil, took bike to greyhound track all week.

Da protected the confidentiality of his finances like an animal protects its young. He never discussed it with Ma. She in turn looked after the lodger money, and he almost never interfered. A couple of times when he was broke and knew there was a sure thing running at some race meeting, he dropped enough hints so that Ma would loan him from the lodger money. Other than that, they kept their finances strictly independent. It was quite probable that Ma didn't know he'd paid off my student loan. It didn't really matter now. What mattered was it was too late to pay it back. No, that wasn't what mattered. That was a lie. What upset me now was that I hadn't gone up to the house and said, "Thanks, Da, for paying off my student loan." I wanted to have the money in my hand and give it to him when I said it, which was foolish, because all he would have wanted was a thank-you. I would have to live with the regret.

I wondered, could his secrets have made him sick? Could they have killed him? You're as sick as your secrets, I heard Ma once say. Keeping a confidence was a great virtue, too. It protected the vulnerable. Da had spent a lifetime doing it. His days of bottling things up were over.

I got off the bus and wandered into the depot out of the sleet. Benjy of the cracked arse was where I'd left him five hours before. He was at a table by himself. He got excited when he saw me and called me over.

— Jesus, you must love us—he said.

I decided not to tell him my news. I didn't want to spoil his break.

— You look very pale, are you all right?—he said.

— I'm fine—I said.

He grabbed up his cigarette box from the table and with his

chubby fingers released one into his mouth. Before he closed the pack again, I saw my hand reach across the table and take one. It felt perfect. The movement of the hand, the filter between the lips, the white tube of comfort, the lighting up followed by the red glow and the explosion of smoke in my mouth. It was eight years since I'd put a cigarette between my lips. The smoke should have choked me. Instead, it felt like I'd found a long-lost friend. My brain told me that I hated cigarettes, my body felt peculiarly alive. My brain said cigarette smoke kills, my body felt like I'd gotten a limb back. I sucked more smoke into my mouth and swallowed it. The taste in my mouth brought me back eight years to my last cigarette. Brought me back thirty years to my first cigarette. Brought me back to a time when Da was alive. I felt dizzy, I don't know if it was the smoke or the thoughts in my head, but I thanked Benjy and made for the door and the fresh air. At the last moment, I diverted to the toilet. I found an empty cubicle and plonked down on the seat. I bent over and stared at the ground and thought about Da's toilet at the end of the garage, where he studied the horses and picked all his best winners. It was his Archimedes seat, the only place where he got time to himself, away from the world. Time to study form and time to work on a system to beat the bookies. You were nowhere without a system. With a system you could conquer the world. One day he would find the formula to make that real. He would be as famous as Archimedes.

I sent more smoke to my brain and felt like I was on a ship. When my head stopped rolling from side to side, I realized the cigarette had nothing to do with me. It was Da. Pure, unadulterated Da. He'd stopped smoking in 1948, the year he married Ma. He had been eleven years off them when he lit up one Sunday after dinner. Ma blamed Doris for Da going back on the cigarettes. Ma blamed Doris for a lot of things. There was always tension in the house when Doris was around. It started before she came and went on while she was here and after she left. Doris lived in Blackburn, Lancashire, and she was coming to stay with us the summer Da went back on the cigarettes. As soon as he reached over and plucked one from Ma's Sweet Afton pack, she said:

— That's because of Doris.

Within a week, he was smoking ten a day, and Ma said:

— That's definitely Doris.

I wondered, would she come over for the funeral? She hadn't been to Dublin for several years. I wondered where she was and what she was doing. Maybe she was reading one of Da's letters. He wrote to her all the time. As regularly as he recorded his financial transactions, he wrote to Doris. Her replies came like clockwork. The envelopes were always the same, small cream squares with the image of the Queen in the right-hand corner and our address printed in neat block capitals with the word "Eire" underlined at the very bottom. The envelopes were fat, because Doris squeezed so many folded pages into such a small space. Da saved reading the letters for his Archimedes seat, and when he returned to the kitchen he would give Ma the news and she would pretend not to care. It was hard to fathom that he would never write a letter again.

I dropped the cigarette butt between my knees into the toilet pan. The rasp of the burning tip hissing to extinction sounded like a stifled human cry. I thought of a soul descending into hell. I watched the butt fragment, the tobacco spilling out onto the watery grave. I hated myself for having the thought about hell, and I pinched myself for my sin. Da was making his journey to heaven, if he wasn't there already—pinch, pinch, pinch.

I heard the main door of the toilet open, and I could tell it was Benjy by the footsteps and the cough. I heard him pee into the metal urinal, and I almost fell off my perch when he bellowed out at the top of his voice:

— Passengers for Dublin, board the bus.

I hurried back to my seat and tried to get comfortable. The saliva in my mouth tasted like pure nicotine. I swallowed hard and felt a sudden remorse for having smoked a cigarette. I said the "Our Father" in my head. It was a great standby in moments of guilt. I finished the prayer and felt guilty I hadn't offered it up for the repose of Da's soul. "Forgive us our trespasses." That was the way with guilt, it begat itself. I said one for Da. "As we forgive those who trespass against us." I added another for Ma, and when I'd finished that I felt I had to throw one in for Doris as well. One for Ireland and one for England. One for the Republic and one for the Monarchy. Catholic and Protestant as one, in perfect harmony. Amen.

3

I stepped off the Derry bus at ten o'clock and went straight to the family home on Carleton Road. It was packed with people talking about Da in the past tense. Nothing in the sitting room had been touched since two o'clock. It had been preserved intact, just like the scene of a murder. My only thought in the world was to hold Ma, which I did, and all she wanted to do, and did, was point to the spot on the floor where she'd found him lying. Over and over again she stretched out her arms and made the shape of his body on the floor. His head towards the door and his feet under the table with the chair on its side. The newspaper on the table spread out on the racing page, and beside it his good pen that he used to mark the day's results.

Ma went through the story from half past one that day. She'd gone to the butcher's for his lamb chop, and she'd stopped by the fruit-and-veg to buy a turnip. On her way back up the street she'd met Mrs. O'Kelly, the next-door neighbor, and they chatted for about ten minutes. That was her first mistake. When she came back into the house, she went straight to the kitchen and started to peel the turnip. That was her second mistake. She heard the radio giving out the racing results, and she knew it wasn't normal, because Da's comments—"ya bastard, the lousy swine"—were missing. She finished peeling the turnip and was about to put the chop under the grill when she decided to ask Da if he wanted a second vegetable. She walked into the sitting room and found him lying on the floor. His eyes were open, but there was no life in them. His body was still and his lips were blue, and she just knew it was too late to do anything, and she rang 999 and didn't remember what she said, but she cursed herself for going to the shops, cursed herself for chatting to Mrs. O'Kelly, and cursed herself for going into the kitchen on her return. She waited with him until the ambulance men came, and she remembered starting an act of contrition in his ear, but she didn't remember finishing it, because she started to give him mouth-to-mouth resuscitation, only his head was the wrong way, and she couldn't turn him over because he was so heavy, and she started to cry because she was too late, he was dead, why was she not there to save him?

I tried to console Ma, as we all did, but my words were no comfort to her. All I could do was listen and nod my head as she launched into the story that began with her fatal decision to go to the butcher's and ended with her kneeling over him and trying to breathe life into him, helplessly trying to breathe life into him.

— His feet were just where the leg of the chair is now—Ma pointed out—and his head was right there.

She had the exact spot fixed in her mind, and her hand went out to it, like she could still caress his face. It was hard to believe he had lain dead there only hours before. The room was alive with people, eating sandwiches and drinking tea and whiskey. They were standing on the same navy carpet that had been his death sheet. He had laid the carpet himself, his fingerprints were on every tack that held it down. His blood was on it, too, a small drop at the spot where Ma was pointing. I imagine it had trickled from his nose when he hit the floor. I wondered had he fallen hard, or had he merely slipped to his knees and nestled down. The chair suggested it had been a gentle fall. A gentle death. Ma was leaving the chair in its place so she could tell the story as the family gathered. When she'd finished telling me, Uncle John arrived and the story started all over again.

— The first mistake I made was chatting to Mrs. O'Kelly—Ma berated herself.

I got up to let Uncle John sit beside her and wandered over to the table. I put my hand on his pen and let the tips of my fingers feel its shape. He'd touched it earlier that day. He'd marked the results with it, as he'd done every day, recording them as faithfully as a monk transcribing the scriptures. He had luscious, decisive handwriting. The racing page was a work of art when he'd finished with it. First, second, and third, with starting prices and tote dividends, all marked with unflinching accuracy. Only today it was unfinished, the strokes of his pen were missing, he never got to finish out his page. The last result he'd marked was the two o'clock from Southwell, a five-furlong sprint at the all-weather track, not his favorite type of race. He'd put a one beside the winner, No Submission, and that was it. No second, no third, and no starting prices. No Submission was the last thing he saw and the last thing he heard. No Submission, and then his heart exploded. No Submission, and he slipped from his chair to the floor and banged his nose with a thud against the carpet.

He loved dying. He loved falling to his knees like he'd been shot in the back. Or holding his stomach like he'd taken an

Apache arrow. It was how he acted out cowboy films for us. Gunfights and ambushes, heroism and cowardice, bandits and chaps, all leading to slow, pain-free deaths on the sitting-room floor as we children watched in wonder while he told us to look after the town when he was gone. Sometimes he embraced that dying so completely, we pinched him in terror until his eyes opened and he came back to life.

He always said that no one on earth could die or kill like Gary Cooper. According to Da, he was the greatest cowboy who ever lived, he was the greatest in his dying and in his living, too. He carried his past in his haunted face like a good cowboy should. He was a man of few words who eschewed violence, but when it was required, he let his guns do the talking. That's how it was in *High Noon*. No one could hold a candle to Gary Cooper in that, and no one could hold a candle to Da when he acted it out for us. He always started off with the singing:

> — *Do not forsake me, oh, my darling*
> *On this our wedding day.*

From there to the finale when he saves the town, it was tension all the way. When he told the story, we wanted Gary Cooper to save the town, but it always seemed he saved it too quickly, because we never wanted it to end. Perhaps he thought of Gary Cooper in that moment after he marked the result. Perhaps he remembered the Metropole Cinema, where he first saw it. He may have remembered Doris, because it was she he'd brought with him that night. Maybe it wasn't Doris but Ma in her wedding outfit and him beside her, arm in arm, just like Grace Kelly and Gary Cooper.

I listened to Ma go through her litany of mistakes and I knew there was nothing she could have done, even if she'd been in the room at the time of his collapse. He was dead by the time he hit the floor. There was no sign of a struggle, all the signs were of a quiet surrender, a gentle leaving. After he'd marked the racing result, his time had come as surely as if he'd been shot through the heart. There was no point in saying any of this to Ma, because she was too caught up in telling her story and having to tell it. Uncle John listened and comforted her as best he could.

Shea rang and spoke to Ita before Ma came on the phone and poured her grief down the line. He was at the airport in Chicago, about to board a flight for Dublin. Ma promised to keep the sitting room exactly as it was until he saw the scene for himself. She passed the phone to me, and Shea asked me where Da was. It took me a minute to realize he meant the body. I told him it was in the mortuary of the Mater Hospital. Shea thought I should get up there, that Da would need the company, because his soul would take twelve hours to pass over to the other side. It was half past eleven, nine and a half hours since his death and two and a half hours left for his spirit journey, if Shea was right. In other circumstances I might have argued the point, but death is not a time for unbelief or uncertainty. If Da was afraid of the journey ahead, I wanted to be with him and hold his hand. I replaced the receiver and made straight for the Mater Hospital.

The mortuary was full of the sound of the rosary. Auntie Anne was leading Auntie Marie and Auntie Lily in the sorrowful mysteries. Sisters praying for a dead brother. Uncle Paddy was there, too, he'd been Da's best man. Petrus and Patricius. They made the familiar prayers sound mournful. "Hail Mary" after "Hail Mary," the foundation stone of the rosary. Decade after decade building steps of prayer to heaven. Then they got onto the beatitudes, like secret Catholic prayers hidden in a vault and taken out for solemn occasions such as this.

— *Queen assumed into heaven, pray for us*
  Queen conceived without sin, pray for us
  Queen of patriarchs, pray for us
  Queen of martyrs, pray for us
  Ark of the covenant, pray for us
  Mirror of justice, pray for us
  Virgin most pure, pray for us
  Virgin most venerable, pray for us
  Virgin most renowned, pray for us
  Virgin most admirable, pray for us
  Mother most merciful, pray for us
  Mother most amiable, pray for us
  Mother of Christ, pray for us
  Star of the sea, pray for us.

When the mantra was finished, they retired from the mortuary and left me alone with Da. I kissed his marble forehead and held his cold hands. I knew he would never be warm again. I told him not to be afraid, that I would stay with him. I told him I would be with him until the journey was over. I closed my eyes the better to feel his spirit, only I felt nothing. There was no sense of him about. I conjured up a picture of him and squeezed his hands. I couldn't find his wavelength. I searched and searched for him, but it was no good. I willed myself into his psyche, but there was no hint of his presence. I offered him words of reassurance the whole time, but he wasn't there. Finally, I opened my eyes and, looking down at him, I realized he was gone. I looked over the contours of his face, and there was no distress there. He wasn't with me, I knew that, he was in a faraway place and he wasn't coming back.

My first thought was that he'd prepared for his leaving. His death had come as a shock to us, but he'd been ready for it. He'd chosen his moment and he'd left. He had no thought or desire to linger, because his work was finished. He'd marked his last racing result and submitted to his fate, literally and metaphorically. By the time Ma had found him, he was on his way to the spirit world. I had friends on the other side that I talked to regularly. Mil Fleming I spoke to almost every day, and Peter Adair less frequently but feeling no less real for that. I could touch Mil's spirit at will and I did (what a source of good advice she was), but I knew, standing in that mortuary, I would never talk to Da again. Whatever part of the spirit world he'd journeyed to had no communication line to earth. There were millions of things I wanted to tell him, and I'd rehearsed them on the bus. I could still say the words, but I would never know if he heard them or not, because he'd left my orbit for good.

We couldn't take Da's body back to the house to wake him, because the medical authorities needed to perform a postmortem. We wanted to take him home for the weekend, but they wouldn't release the body until they had established the cause of death. We sat in the house discussing the options when Shea arrived in from Chicago, and Ma got all upset as she launched into the story of how she'd found him on the floor and how she might have saved him had she not met Mrs. O'Kelly and had she not peeled the turnip for his dinner. I told Shea he was dead when he hit the floor, and he believed me, but it was no consolation to Ma. What did console her was the fact that we were all home and under the one roof—Shea, Ita, me, Johnny, Gerard, and Paul—her six surviving children. Frankie was above in Glasnevin, and the grave would be opened soon to take Da. We'd come home to bury him.

The result of the postmortem came quicker than expected. We were surprised to learn that the cause of death was viral pneumonia. He must have been ill for some time and said nothing. According to the doctors, the end would have been very sudden, and no medical intervention would have saved him. A black cloud visibly lifted from around Ma. She picked up the chair that had been on its side and put it back in its place. She folded the newspaper with the racing result and put it away along with his good pen. Then she told us that she wasn't up to having the body home, but that we would wake it instead in the funeral home on the Malahide Road.

We sat around the coffin in a big circle—children, grand-children, daughters-in-law, son-in-law, Ma—and we cried for our loss, which was great. We cried for the repose of his soul, and when the crying was over it was time for laughter. Paul said we'd forgotten the most important thing in our grief.

— He's looking down at us now and he's calling us bastards—Paul went on.

— Why is he calling us bastards?—Ma wanted to know.

— What did we forget to give him?—Paul wanted to know.

Paul looked around the circle of bewildered faces. No one knew. Paul knew no one knew. He plucked the newspaper from his pocket and shook it at us.

— We forgot to give him yesterday's results.

There was a momentary silence before Ma jumped in.

— You'd better read them out to him, so, Paulie.

With Ma's comment the room burst into laughter. Paul opened the paper and read out the results in a perfect imitation of Da's voice.

— Two-thirty. First, Go Ballistic. Oh, Jesus, oh, Je-sus. I was waiting on that bastard and I missed him—Paul ranted at us, just like Da.

Ma couldn't control herself. None of us could. Racing re-sults never seemed so funny before. After the results, the stories started. Ma told one about herself and Da in Paris when he had a tip for a horse but couldn't get a bet on. She traipsed after him from one side of Paris to the other, from the Right Bank to the Left Bank and up and down the Seine in search of a bookie's shop. Ma wanted to give up, but Da knew the French loved racing so there had to be a betting shop in their kip of a capital city. Finally, his persistence was repaid and he saw a sign—a great big painting of a horse's head on the gable wall of a house—and he knew his luck was in. He ran all the way, armed with his bet, and went inside to get it on. It took him a minute to realize they only dealt in dead horses, not live ones—it was, in fact, a butcher's shop for horsemeat.

For two hours we laughed and cried over Da, and the funeral director peeped in once or twice because he'd never seen a wake like it. We celebrated Da's life in that odd room with the heavy scent of flowers and the candles burning, we celebrated with laughter in a place designed for tears. I had never felt such sadness and joy side by side, never thought that loss could be so funny, never realized that laughter could be so spiritual. The only surprise was that Da didn't get up and join in the fun. If his spirit was ever likely to be among us again, it was those hours around his coffin in the funeral home. The truth was, we could remember him, and always would, but he was gone to a part of the spirit world from where he was never coming back.

Two days later, a large crowd stood around the open grave in Glasnevin Cemetery on a cold January morning. I'd stood in the same place three times before. In 1963 for my grandfather James, in 1967 for my brother Frankie, and in 1980 for my grandmother Elizabeth. Da, who had been the great keeper of this grave, had reached his time. As the official church prayers came to an end, Johnny raised a trombone to his lips and blew a note. The members of his jazz band followed his lead, and the sound of music filled the cemetery. Smiles of recognition broke out everywhere as people recognized Da's song, "Frankie and Johnny." I hummed it in my head and remembered him singing it on Christmas night barely three weeks before. Johnny and his band played him on his way to join Frankie. When the music finished and the people started to disperse, Shea and I went over and asked the gravediggers for their shovels. Paul and Gerard removed the covering from the grave, and we shoveled clay in on top of Da's coffin until it was covered. Then Ita and Johnny took a turn, followed by Gerard and Paul. We kept shoveling until the task was complete and there was nothing left to do.

Ma decided it was time to tell Doris. I bought her a nice ballpoint pen for the task. She wrote as neatly as she could, because she would want Doris to think only the best of her. There were many times over the years she'd wanted to write to her. Times when Da lost the run of himself, gambled his wages on a sure thing that got the mallet and plunged the house into despair. Other occasions when he went on a hunger strike because Ma could take no more and stood up to him. This was the Peter Doris never saw but Ma lived with day in and day out.

Throughout the years, Ma resisted putting the truth on paper. Deep down she knew it would reflect badly on her. She'd made her bed and she was determined to lie in it. Ma knew intuitively that to criticize Da was to make herself vulnerable. Instead, she welcomed Doris into the bosom of the family, from where she could keep a close eye on her. In between visits, she was happy to let Da loose with his letters. Now she was writing to her rival for the first time.

Dear Doris, I'm very sorry to inform you that Peter passed away on the 14th of last month.

She kept the letter short and to the point. She knew Doris would come to pay her respects. She was going to suggest a small hotel in Gardiner Street, not far from the ferry terminal, where Doris could stay overnight. That said, she would never forgive herself if Doris came to Dublin and was mugged on her way to or from the cemetery. So she did the Christian thing and offered her the single bed upstairs in the spare room.

I barely recognized Doris when I opened the hall door to her. She looked old-fashioned. I brought her into the hall and took her hat and coat, but she held on to her bag for dear life. She was wearing a black dress with a stand-alone cream knitted collar. It gave her the appearance of a monarch. From the neck down, she was Elizabeth I. From the neck up, she was a double for Andy Warhol. She had large, piercing eyes and a shock of white hair.

Ma came out and shook her timidly by the hand. They talked about the weather. From there they were into the tribulations of crossing the Irish Sea. They entered the sitting room and sat opposite one another at the table. Doris castigated Ma for going to so much trouble with the sandwiches. I poured out her tea, but not before she put her milk and sugar in first. Ma's best china was out for the occasion. Doris had come a long way to pay her respects, and Ma wanted to treat her properly. She wanted to treat her as Da would have wished. He was gone to his eternal rest, and there was no point in perpetuating bad feeling. Perhaps they could even be friends, now that Peter was gone.

— I tidied up the grave, it were a bit of a mess—
Doris said.

It was impossible not to sense the veiled criticism in Doris's words. Or perhaps it was said out of nervousness. It was seventeen years since she'd been to Dublin, seventeen years since she'd seen Ma, and she was trying to break the ice with her.

      — I put the roses on the grave, as I promised—Doris said.

      I could see Ma was struggling to make sense of all this.

      — What do you mean?—she asked.

      — Peter asked me to put red and white roses on his grave—she said.

Ma didn't know what to say or where to turn. I could see the shock in her face. There was defiance there, too, of course. Doris was out to prove how great her love for Peter was. For a moment, I thought Ma was going to show her the door. Instead, she smiled at her guest and pretended everything was fine with the world. The charge between them was electrifying. For the first time since his death, Da's spirit was present in the house. It was there in the tug-o'-war between Doris and Anna.

Ma put on a brave face while her guest was in the house. She answered all her questions without going into details. She went through the story of finding him on the floor but she did it in a perfunctory sort of way. She was much happier talking about the bingo and the weather. She smiled and showed Doris to her room. Behind the façade, she was seething.

The following morning, she bade Doris farewell at the hall door. Ma then put on her coat and scarf and instructed me to drive her to Glasnevin Cemetery. I drove in the front gate and followed the markings to plot HJ 223½. It was six weeks since we'd buried Da. The funeral wreaths were still piled around the grave. A space had been cleared away in the center, about where his heart would be. On it lay a fresh bunch of red and white roses. The blooms had not yet opened. I picked them up and counted them. There were forty-seven in all. It seemed like an arbitrary number and didn't make any particular sense.

      — Why forty-seven? I asked Ma.

— Because this has been going on for forty-seven years, son, and it's still not over, Ma replied through lips quivering in anger.

The war of the roses. One stem for every year of its duration. A war that had begun in 1947 and was still raging in 1994. Ma reached across, took the flowers from me and threw them on the path. She marched back to the car and got in. I followed and took her back home in an angry silence.

I had to meet Doris, but I didn't know what I would say to her. On the one hand, I didn't want Ma being upset by her visits to Da's grave and her floral tributes to him. On the other hand, I was curious to get to the bottom of it all.

4

I was sitting in a hotel room in Manchester, giddy like a child, fumbling through bits of paper, looking for Doris's telephone number. I was excited about seeing her, in a forbidden sort of way. I felt like I was stepping back into Da's life, and the reward was some extra time with him. How could I say no to this, however painful the truth might prove to be? I went through my pile of papers—old receipts, business cards, bank lodgments, betting dockets, dental appointments—and examined them front and back. My pockets are always full of bits of paper too valuable to throw away. There was no sign of Doris's number among the elite. I opened out a bookies' docket. It was a ten-pound win bet on No Submission. The horse had run several times since Da's death and had won quite a few of its races. This docket represented one of its losses, and I'd held on to it because I was superstitious about throwing it away. I thought it would bring me bad luck. There was absolutely no sense to it, of course, but it satisfied some insane logic in my head. Da wrote "Toby Jug" on the back of his dockets in the belief it would bring a blessing to his horses. I have no idea why he believed those words had magical powers. I held on to the bookies' docket because No Submission was the last horse he'd marked before he left us. I had not felt his presence since, except when Doris turned up in Dublin. I wanted to meet her to renew that feeling. I knew Ma had the number, but I couldn't call and ask her. I'd have had to explain what I was doing, and it would feel like too much of a betrayal. In the end, I called directory enquiries, asked for a number for Doris Johnson, Miss, gave Victoria Street, Blackburn, as the address, and apologized that I didn't know the house number. Twenty seconds later, a machine voice gave me the number and asked me did I want to be connected. It seemed too sudden, and I put down the receiver. I hadn't worked out what I would say. I wasn't even sure if Doris would want to see me. What would I say if she refused? I prepared myself for a rejection and made the call. She answered immediately.

    — I've been waiting to hear from you, when are you coming to see me?

I was relieved and excited.

    — I'm coming today, if that's all right?—I said.

    — Of course it's all right—she said.

    — How long will it take by taxi?—I asked.

I could hear the gasp of astonishment at the other end of the phone.

    — You'll do no such thing, it's too expensive to come by taxi.—She was affronted.

    — The money's not a problem, Doris.

    — You'll take a train, young man, that's what you'll do. It's cheaper and it's quicker.—Her tone was definite.

In normal circumstances I'd have argued the point, but

since she was facilitating me, I was less inclined to make a principle of it.

— If you want me to take the train, I'll take the train—I submitted.

She gave me my instructions, and I set out to meet her. I bought a return ticket at Victoria Station, Manchester, and when I found the platform I was the only person there. When the train arrived, it was completely empty. It felt like a dream where everyone had disappeared but the machines still worked. Along the way, people joined the train, but they didn't speak. Everyone kept to themselves, preserving the surreal atmosphere. I stepped off the train at my stop, and Doris sprinted along the platform and threw her arms around me. I'd never been hugged with such passion by an elderly lady before. Her embrace was strong, with the vigor of someone half her age. We gave the ghosts on the train something out of the ordinary to look at. Doris held me as though I'd been lost and had come home, she held me like I was hers. I held her, too, for how could I not respond to her warmth? I wrapped her small frame in my arms and protected her. I put my hand up to the back of her head and stroked her white hair. She squeezed me tight and let her head nestle against my chest. We stood there holding each other until long after the train had gone. Once or twice I tried to relax my hold, but Doris wasn't letting go. Finally, she pulled back and reached into her pocket for a hankie. She wiped her eyes, and I could feel the stain of her tears on my shirt.

— Look what I've done—she exclaimed.—I've gone and ruined your shirt.

She pawed at it with her hankie, and try as I might to reassure her, she berated herself for the offense. Having run out of ways of apologizing, finally, she grabbed my right arm with her two hands and we set off up the hill towards Victoria Street. Along the way she acknowledged the stares of her friends and neighbors, her postman, butcher, a district nurse, and a man in a suit who looked like a vet. She made no attempt to introduce me, but I could tell she was proud from the breadth of her smile. As we walked up the hill, I understood she'd insisted on the train precisely to parade me in public. By the time we reached the terraced red-bricked house, almost an hour later, my feet were sorry I hadn't taken a taxi.

It was nearly forty years since I'd seen the inside of 15 Victoria Street. I was a six-year-old boy, and Da had brought me over to see Manchester United play at Old Trafford. We'd come out to visit after the match, and I remembered it as full of life. It seemed older and sadder now. Where had all that life gone to? Did it reside in the walls and timbers of the house? Could we encourage it to come out and play if we were quiet enough? Doris chose the armchair I was to sit in, it was a sepia brown, low to the ground, with a piece of pink lace for the head and two matching pieces for the arms. On a small table beside it sat an ashtray with a picture of O'Connell Street complete with Nelson's Pillar (it had been blown up by the IRA in 1966). There were other mementos of Ireland, including a miniature Blarney Castle and a wall hanging with "Bless This House" written across it. Over the fireplace was a photograph of Doris and Da taken at a dress dance, and beside it, as if to give it legitimacy, hung a coronation photograph of the Queen. On the sideboard, shoulder to shoulder, sat two radios, each in its own mahogany casing.

— Why do you need two radios?—I asked her.

— Why do you think, you silly moo!—she replied.

I hadn't the faintest idea. I scrunched up my face as I do when I'm thinking, and I must have looked a sight, because Doris laughed right at me.

— One is to hear you, silly moo—she chortled and

pointed to the bigger of the two—this is my Dublin radio, tuned to RTÉ, and I've heard you on it once or twice.

The other radio was tuned to the BBC, and she worked them simply by plugging in and out of the wall socket as required. It meant she never had to adjust the tuning. RTÉ was her favorite, because she preferred the Irish accent to the English accent. She loved the sound of a genuine Irish voice, she thought it very musical. I thanked her for the compliment and she burst out laughing again.

— Your father will never be dead while you're alive—she said.

It was the nicest thing anyone had said to me since his death. I could have returned the compliment, but her love for Da was so palpable, I didn't need to. He was alive for her, that was plain. Indeed, she'd had no experience of his death, she hadn't seen his corpse or been present at the burial. Her love transcended the grave, and it was humbling for me to know that she had loved him so much but had had no chance to speak of it. I looked at her and wondered how she had sustained this love over more than four decades: sustained it imprisoned within these walls when Da was living with us in Dublin. I thought how lonely her life must have been without him, living vicariously off the radio, waiting for his letters in the post, composing her replies, and sending them in small white envelopes sealed with Sellotape on the back. I remembered her letters and her parcels at Christmas. It had never crossed my mind they were love letters she'd written to Da, or maybe I'd known and suppressed it, because I only ever wanted him to love Ma.

— Did Da love you?—I asked her.

— Oh, yes. He loved me very much—she said.

I had no reason to disbelieve her. I sat back in the chair and asked her why she had come to Ireland in the first place.

I was intrigued by Ireland from the time I was a little girl. My father thought it was a backward little country, and the more he criticized it, the more fascinated I became. I heard Count John McCormack sing "I'll Take You Home Again, Kathleen" on the radio, and as far as I was concerned, he was singing to me. I was Kathleen, and his voice beckoned me. It sounds silly, but that's what I believed. I felt like I'd been there in a previous life and I had to return. Father said the Irish drank too much, were foul-mouthed and devoid of any culture. When he went on a rant, I just closed my ears and conjured up John McCormack in my head.

In the summer of 1945, I announced I was taking a holiday in Ireland. It was just after my twenty-first birthday. I found a guesthouse in Bray from an advert in the local paper and sent off a booking deposit of ten shillings. When the confirmation came back in the post, all hell broke loose.

— Do you know what's happening in Europe, do you, girl?— Father wanted to know. He were fuming. I held my nerve and said nothing. Winifred, my mother, was sitting right where you are. She asked Father to pour her a sherry, and she hardly ever drank. Celia, my younger sister, was standing over by the door. She were the pet. When Father shouted at me, she answered.

— Do you know what's happening lass?—Father said.

— There's a war going on, Father—Celia answered.

— It's not just any war, it's a world war—he bellowed.

That evening, a policeman came round to the house and told me I wasn't to travel. His name was Alex Whiteley, and he were a friend of Dad's. They stood over my shoulder while I wrote to the guesthouse asking for the deposit back. The writing paper were wet from the tears running down my face. I wanted Father to put his arms around me, but he reserved all that for Celia. She didn't defy him at every hand's turn, you see. I never did what I was told, and he never showed me any love.

I never stopped dreaming of crossing the Irish Sea. When the booking deposit was returned, I kept the envelope and the ten-shilling note under my pil-

low. I'd take it out at night and look at the stamp. It was a map of Ireland. It looked like a teddy bear to me. I'd take out the orange ten-shilling note and put it under my nose and imagine it smelt like Ireland.

In the winter of 1947, I booked a holiday at Red Island in Skerries. Mother couldn't see the attraction of it when we had Pontins in our own back yard. Father wanted to know what Skerries offered that they didn't have in Blackpool, Brighton, or Southend.

— They have ballroom-dancing competitions—I told him.

— You can't dance—he said—you're too awkward for dancing.

— I'm a good dancer—I said—so stop saying I can't dance. Stop saying it.

— Don't contradict your father or you'll not be let go to bloody Ireland

I'd stood up to him, and for the first time in my life I didn't apologize. I didn't back down. I was going to Ireland and that was that. When the time came, I couldn't believe I was standing by the front door getting my final instructions.

— Don't talk to any strange men, and watch your English accent, and look out for IRA men following you, and stay inside camp at all times, and don't go into Dublin on your own.

It were like I was being asked to swallow the flipping Bible. I caught the night train to Holyhead, got on the Dún Laoghaire boat, and stood on deck for the entire journey. Several strange men tried to speak to me, and I successfully ignored them all. When the customs official asked me had I anything to declare I pretended I was deaf and dumb. I took the train to Amiens Street and arrived there at 7:20 a.m. The Skerries train wasn't until 8:30 a.m. I had over an hour to wait. Mother had packed a flask of tea and corned-beef sandwiches. I thought of having them and looked around for a seat. On second thoughts, I decided to buy the train ticket first. I approached the booth, dragging my cases with me. The man behind the counter smiled at me.

— Can you manage?—he asked.

I looked him full in the face. It was Peter. Your dad. He had a lovely *voice. I thought he was Count John McCormack. I had never seen Count John McCormack, but this was how I pictured him. A full round face with red cheeks, black hair parted on the left, no grease.*

— You should get your boyfriend to carry them—he said.

He were very cheeky, even then. I couldn't help myself laughing at his cheek. I asked him for a single to Red Island, Skerries. He asked me to repeat myself, I don't know why, maybe it was my accent. I just started blabbering. Like I couldn't form proper words. Maybe it was the tension of the travel and being afraid to speak to anyone. I think I managed to say "a single to Skerries."

— I can give you a return for the same price as a single—he offered.

I didn't know what to say, I thought he was going to start singing. I watched his mouth, waiting for the words: "I'll Take you Home Again, Kathleen." He pulled out a brown ticket and stamped it. Valid for three months, it said. He pushed it across the counter towards me.

— The train leaves at eight-thirty from platform five—he said.

— Where's platform five?—I asked.

He disappeared, and in a few seconds he was outside the booth, picking up my cases.

— Come on, I'll show you—he said.

He took me to the platform and found a seat. I asked him about Count John McCormack. Peter told me he was from Athlone, that he had lived in a house in Blackrock, and that he had heard him sing "Panis Angelicus" in 1932. I was speechless that the count had sung for him, and he let me be impressed before he told me that there were a half a million others there besides himself. I loved the way he told stories. He had a great way with words. His voice reminded me of bathwater. I just wanted to sit there and listen to it, like sitting in hot water and not wanting to move. At one point I offered him a sandwich. I asked him what his favorite filling was and he said corned beef. He couldn't believe it when I took a corned-beef sandwich out of my bag. He refused my offer of tea at first, but I persisted until he changed his mind. He swirled it around his mouth and washed down the stray bits of bread. I handed him a handkerchief, and he wiped his fingers and lips with it.

When the train came, Peter put me safely in a seat with my luggage. I had been warned not to talk to strangers and I had spent over an hour in the company of the first man who'd given me a civil word. We'd shared a picnic together. He'd wiped his mouth in my hankie.

— Would you like my address in Blackburn?—I asked him.

I didn't want him to leave. In desperation, I scribbled out my address and handed it to him. He shouted his address in Dublin at me:

— I live in 5a Friary Avenue, Smithfield.

He got off the train as the whistle sounded, and he stood on platform five. I came to the window and stuck my head out.

— We have a dance on Saturday night, if you're free.

I wasn't sure if he'd heard me or not, so I shouted it again. Then I sat down and hoped to God there weren't any members of the IRA on board the train.

Doris broke off from her account to offer me lunch. I didn't want her to stop. I wanted her to continue with her story that made him vulnerable and conniving. I had only known him as a father, and as a father he had always seemed a mythical figure. I always quaked, somehow, in his presence. Doris painted him with feet of clay, she humanized him. I could picture his chat-up technique, and I could see myself sitting on the bench doing the exact same thing.

— I've left you sitting there without a bite of food in your tummy—she scolded herself.

She hopped out to the kitchen and got busy. I heard the clatter of plates and the clash of cutlery. I knew what was coming, she was going to offer me corned-beef sandwiches. How was I going to tell her I couldn't stand the sight of corned beef, real or processed? I was like my father in many respects, I even shared some of his eating habits. I had to have a slice of bread and butter washed down with tea after my dinner every day, just like him. One thing I didn't share was his penchant for corned beef. My stomach was doing somersaults at the very thought.

— Do you remember fishing with your father out in Howth?—Doris shouted in at me.

Did I remember, would I ever forget?

— Indeed, I do—I answered.

— Do you remember what you fished for?—she asked.

— Mackerel—I answered—we were always after the mackerel.

I would never forget those expeditions, which ended in such glorious failure. It didn't help that we fished with improvised rods made from broken broom handles and fishing line that was made from leftover twine knotted together and a reel that Da had found in a dump somewhere. We concentrated our efforts along the wall where the boats were tethered. I'd have the rod, Da held the net, and Johnny carried the bucket for the catch. I always wondered why we fished in a place that was full of oil and rubbish.

— Because we're fishing for mackerel—Da would say.

— And why do mackerel like oil and rubbish?—we would say.

— Mackerel are the scavengers of the sea, they only eat shit—Da would say.

Who were Johnny and I to argue with our creator? Da knew everything there was to know about fishing. Yet we never caught a single thing out in Howth, not a mackerel or a fish of any description. We knew there were millions of fish there, because we saw them coming in off the fishing boats. We were doing something wrong, only Da wouldn't admit it. He put it all down to luck. One of us was a Jonah, Johnny or me, and that's why the mackerel didn't bite.

Doris came in from the kitchen with two chairs and set them at the table. She asked me to put up one of the leaves and sit down for my lunch. I did as commanded, and when I pulled out the support leg, it came away in my hand. It was as if it had been waiting to disintegrate. I didn't know what to do. I sat down in my chair and held the leaf up with my knee.

— I have a surprise for you—she said from the kitchen.

Doris came in with the plate and plonked it down in front of me. It wasn't corned beef; indeed, it wasn't a sandwich of any description. It took me a moment to register that it was fish.

— That's the mackerel you never caught out in Howth—Doris beamed down at me.

I was glad it was fish, but my delight was somewhat tempered by the fact that the plate was only staying on the horizontal plane with the help of my knee. What was I to do? Doris was staring at me, waiting for me to pronounce judgment on the mackerel. I put a chunk in my mouth and swallowed quickly.

— It's perfect, just perfect—I said with my mouth full.

Doris sat and watched me. The leaf of the table felt like it weighed about four tons. I was sure she could see the table moving up and down, but if she did, she said nothing. I wolfed down the food as quickly as I could and handed her back my plate. I dropped the leaf and was overcome with a ferocious feeling of nausea. I just had to vomit. I asked her where the toilet was, and she pointed it out to me. When I went to stand up, my knee, which was now numb, went from under me, and I fell down on the floor. I was within a second of leaving the mackerel on the carpet when I hauled myself up and made it to the bathroom. I puked the entire dinner into the toilet bowl, and what missed its intended target found its way onto my jacket and shirt. The smell was noxious, and not even four flushes of the cistern did anything to dispel it. I swore I would never eat mackerel again as long as I lived. I came back to the sitting room and resumed my place on the armchair.

— I knew you'd enjoy that fish—Doris shouted in from the kitchen.

She came back in with a pot of tea and a plate of bread. She smiled at me, and I knew it gave her the greatest pleasure in the world to know that I was my father's son. I plowed into the tea and bread, and she took up the story where she'd left it earlier.

I was the first person into the ballroom on the Saturday night. I didn't mind it was empty, I liked being early for things. Since I was a little girl, I've hated being late for anything. Four men asked me up to dance and I refused them all. I told them I was spoken for. A married man from Yorkshire, he was called Bill and Vera was his wife, he persecuted me that much I said yes, finally. Worst thing I could have done. He followed me the whole night. I felt sorry for Vera, to be honest, running after him. He had no shame, that one. At eleven o'clock I went back to my chalet and got in under the covers. I could hear the music and the dancing and the laughing. I wanted to be there. I didn't want to be in bed feeling sorry for myself. It were supposed to be a holiday. It were my first Saturday in Ireland. I wanted to kill Peter for not turning up. I hardly knew him, and I wanted him dead for letting me down. It were only a passing thought. In my heart I knew he wanted to be there. I pulled the covers up over my head and wrapped them around my ears, but I could still hear the music. I couldn't make it go away. In my mind, I pictured him coming into the hall and looking for me. All around the edge he went and back again, looking to see if I were there. It was so real, I had to get out of bed and go back. My dress was all crumpled and my hair was a state. I splashed my face, combed my hair, straightened out the creases, and headed for the ballroom. Just as I got there, Bill and Vera appeared out of the darkness. They'd been all around the camp looking for me. Bill was very worried I wasn't having a good time.

— It's a gents' choice, and you're going to dance with me—Bill said.

— You'd best do as he says, lass, he's the boss—Vera added.

With that, I turned tail and went back to my chalet and got into my bed. All I could do was lie there and imagine how things might have been different. On my way back through Dublin, I stopped off at the station. I went to the booth, but there was no sign of Peter. I asked after him and they told me he was out sick. What do you know but when I got back from my holiday there's a letter sitting on the table waiting for me. I knew something were up from my father's glum expression.

— Someone's writing to you—he said.—I hope it's not trouble.

I took the letter and went upstairs. I sat on the bed and stared at the envelope. The handwriting were very distinctive. I knew it were Peter's hand. Inside was the sorry tale of how he'd turned up at the Red Island dance and I wasn't there. He'd been drinking in Madigan's Pub in town because he'd won some money on the horses. He'd arrived late at the dance, expecting to find me there because his luck was in. I'd brought the good fortune with the horses, you see. He looked all over the ballroom for me, just as I'd imagined from my bed. He was so disappointed I'd stood him up. He wanted to search the camp but didn't want to find me wrapped in the arms of another. He envied the man of my affections, whoever he was. He couldn't let things go without dropping a line to say how glad he was to have met me. Not forgetting the corned-beef sandwiches and the chat. And he looked forward to a reply if my heart was still free.

The letter made me drunk. I'd never been drunk, but this was how I imagined it. His words were stamped on my soul. Count John McCormack had never touched me like this. I wasted no time writing to him at Friary Avenue. I cut a corner of the orange ten-shilling note and put my initials on one side and Peter's on the other. DJ and PS, one on top of the other, the way they were meant to be. I couldn't think of my life any more without thinking of his.

I sent off the letter and waited for a reply, but none came. I waited for weeks and weeks. I were nearly distracted. I wanted to get on a boat and go to Dublin, and I should have done, but I had no one to advise me. There was *no point in saying anything to Mother and Father, they'd have criticized me. Celia was the only one and she didn't believe in love. It was all down to me. I wrote again, and this time I sent it to the train station in Amiens Street. Two weeks later, I got a reply. The letter came from Dundalk. I had to look at a map to see where it was. It were north of Dublin, about halfway to Belfast. He'd been transferred there some time before. His employers had forwarded my letter to him. Unfortunately, he'd never received the earlier correspondence. He'd asked at home, and no one could remember it coming in the door. That was my first suspicion that it had been intercepted. There was someone didn't want Peter receiving that letter. After all, we were supposed to be enemies. He's Irish and I'm English. We were separated by religion and politics. He'd told me his father was a veteran of the 1916 Rising. Trust me to fall for the son of an IRA man! My parents would have committed me if they'd known. I can only suspect his own father would have had him shot, or worse. I was so glad we were above it, and I was so glad to get his reassuring letter. It had been four months since I'd declared my love to him. Four months since I'd told him my heart was his to do with as he pleased. Four months for me to lose him to some-one else. That's what happened, you see, I lost him, and I've lost him again now. I thought I couldn't lose him a second time. I thought my heart couldn't break twice, but it has.*

Her words trailed off into silence. She had stepped back over forty-seven years, and she had brought me with her. She'd in-troduced me to a part of my father's life I hadn't known about. The world, up until this point, had begun with Ma and Da. Nothing had happened before that time. I was now sitting in the presence of someone who could have been his wife. Some-one who knew him before he met Ma. It was a strange, childish feeling, making the world seem full of surprise and at the same time full of danger. I reached out and took her hand in mine, be-cause that's what Da would have done. I held it firmly, because

I wanted her to know she was still loved. I was the physical connection to Da, and he'd left her without saying goodbye. She hadn't kissed his corpse. I was compelled to hold her and to acknowledge, in that moment, that Da had loved her and she had loved him. At the same time, it was hard not to feel it was a betrayal of Ma and the family. The deeper betrayal would have been not to acknowledge Doris's love.

— Who do you think intercepted your letter?—I asked her.

— I don't know. His mother, I suppose, or Anna. Someone who didn't want him to marry me—she said.

I thought about Granny Sheridan. I was afraid of her as a child. She had a reputation of being as tough as old boots. She'd survived the 1916 Rising and Granddad's incarceration in Wales. She'd seen him locked up at the start of the Civil War, leaving her with two young children to mind and another on the way. She'd sacrificed a lot to see an independent Ireland. Was she about to let her son move over and sleep with the enemy? Still, I couldn't see her opening a letter of Da's and living to tell the tale.

— Whoever read it destroyed it, that's all I know—Doris said.

Da discussed everything that went on in the world, but he'd never spoken of his relationship with Doris. It was fascinating to find it shrouded in such intrigue. I had always assumed that Doris was just a friend of the family. I thought Da had met her on one of his many trips to England. He had befriended her and her husband and the friendship had survived her husband's death. She came to stay with us many times in Seville Place and brought her daughter, Amanda, along with her. There was always tension in the house surrounding those visits, and it was only now I understood why. I could still recall, as a child, Ma lifting the sweeping brush over her head and trying to hit Da with it. I remember him grabbing it and her trying to pull it from him. I got in between and told them to stop fighting.

— If she comes, I go—Ma was shouting at him through her sobs.

I knew it had something to do with Doris, because Da was meeting her off the boat. I didn't know as I tried to separate them that she was a rival in Da's affections.

I held Doris's hand and felt a part of the madness. I thought his life had ended when we placed him in the grave in Glasnevin Cemetery. I thought his spirit had left for good when I stood in the mortuary chapel on the day he died. I assumed I would never communicate with him again, and that felt like an awful wrench. Now his life was continuing and I was a part of it. I was exhilarated and afraid, but I had no choice.

My letter reached him at Dundalk Station, and he replied. He wrote to me several times, and he never once mentioned Anna. He talked about the pubs and the town and the dances in some hotel—the Imperial, I think it was called. He went to Dundalk Races once or twice, and he won and then missed work on account of being hung over. He never mentioned Anna once. Never said he'd met anyone. I told him I'd booked Red Island again the following year, and he never said "Don't come." I was traveling on the Wednesday-night boat, and I arranged to see him on the Thursday morning in Amiens Street. Then he wrote and asked me to meet him in Madigan's Pub of North Earl Street on the Friday lunchtime. He drew a map of where it was and put it in with his letter. I was so excited we were going to meet again after the tragedy of the dance the year before.

I turned up at the appointed time, and I went in the bar by mistake, and it were men only. I knew from the looks I received I were in the wrong place. I ducked out and went into the lounge, and he were sitting at the table facing the door. He was with a man of his own age, and he introduced him as Todd Mc-

Donald from the booking office. Peter asked me what I was having to drink, and I said a sherry, because I didn't know what else to order. He went to the counter to get it, and Todd pulled out a chair, and I sat down. Just then a woman came out of the toilet, and I was surprised when she walked over to our table and sat down. Todd made the introductions.

— Anna, this is Doris; Doris, this is Anna—Todd said.

— Are you Todd's girlfriend?—I asked her.

She looked at me like I had a cabbage for a brain.

— Anna is Peter's wife—Todd informed me.

I thought he was joking. I really thought he was pulling my leg. I don't know if I laughed or what I did, but they weren't about to make a fool of me altogether. I was Peter's girlfriend. He was spoken for. His heart were in his letters, and I had them safe in my bag on my knee. I wasn't going to fall for their silly joke. I turned to Anna.

— You're not married to him—I said—you can't be.

— Peter's my husband—she said—I'm his wife.

She weren't joking. She were deadly serious. I felt like she'd taken a dagger and plunged it in my heart. I sat there bleeding to death. I didn't know what to do. I felt like I was two feet tall, sitting on a giant's chair, and I wanted to hide. My face was on fire with embarrassment and rage. I didn't know what to do with my hands or the drink when it came to the table. I didn't know what to do with Peter. I wanted to kill him, of course. He were worse than my father, and that were bad. At least my father had never loved me. Peter had loved me and now he'd taken it away. He'd trampled all over my dreams and made muck of my future.

He suggested the four of us go dancing together. He, Anna, Todd, and myself. The Red Island dance was the suggestion. The young man from the booking office with the red hair and the light-brown freckles thought it was a great idea. I knew then why he'd been brought along. I had no interest in Todd. I had come to Ireland and found what I was looking for, and now it was being taken away from me. Peter pressed me to make up the foursome, but I declined.

— Do you not like dancing?—Anna said.

I loved dancing, but I couldn't tell her, because I wanted to do a fox-trot on her head. If I'd had poison, I would have spiked her drink. I sat there with my head bowed and stared at Anna's ring. We left the pub and walked in formation down Talbot Street, towards the station. I didn't want to go back to Red Island. I didn't want to go home to Blackburn. If there'd been a bus handy, I would have thrown myself under it. I felt completely unwanted.

They walked me up the granite steps to the station. Anna excused herself and went to the toilet. She'd gone twice in the pub and again now. Maybe she was trying to make an opportunity for Peter to say something to me. Perhaps they'd planned it together. If they had, they hadn't told Todd, because he was still standing there smiling over at me the whole time. Eventually, Peter told him to go back to his post. He shook my hand and left.

— Why didn't you tell me about Anna?—I asked Peter.

— I couldn't—he said—I couldn't do it.

— You've made a right fool of me—I said.

— I didn't want to lose you. I was afraid of losing you, that's all—he said.

— So instead of that you humiliate me in front of Anna and your friend—I said.

— I'm sorry—he said—I'm sorry for this awful mess.

He was sorry, I could tell. He knew he'd made a mistake. I could see it in his eyes. He'd made the worst mistake of his life. There was nothing more to be said. Anna came bounding across the black and white tiles towards where we were standing. It was the first time I'd seen her from a distance. She had a very determined walk. She looked like she'd march right into hell and back out again. I realized, too, that she was pregnant. She had that air about her. She was carrying something inside and she was glowing with it. It was Peter's baby, and nothing could take it away from her. I can't say I was happy for her, because I felt she'd taken something away from me. Her happiness was my despair.

Peter, in contrast, looked anything but happy. He should have been over the moon, but he wasn't. He looked like a man with his foot in a snare and he didn't know where to turn. Should he stay where he was or should he pull himself free? They walked me to platform five, past the bench where we'd shared the corned-beef sandwiches. They put me on the Skerries train but didn't come on board. I sat in my seat and didn't look back. I couldn't shake off the feeling that Peter was an unhappy man. First there was the letter, and now the pregnant bride. Had he been forced into marriage? I wondered. Is that why he looked so glum? When I got to Red Island, I started a letter asking all those questions and more. I was angry, and the pen punctured the paper and I had to start again. When I finished, I folded the letter and put it in my bag. It was the only letter I'd written to Peter and would never send. I kept it to remind myself of that awful day, the worst day of my life. I didn't send it because I knew our relationship wasn't over. In some ways, it was only beginning. As he'd said on the platform, he didn't want to lose me. I wasn't about to lose him, either, no matter how long I had to wait.

5

I couldn't ask Ma if she was pregnant getting married. From the beginning of time, she and Da had stared down at us from their wedding photograph on the wall. Peter and Anna on their big day, April 5, 1948. Beside that a second photograph, Peter and Anna with bridesmaid and best man, Dympna and Paddy, Ma's sister and Da's brother, respectively. Da was skinnier then, but Ma hadn't changed an ounce, the passion and fire in her eyes clearly visible. She looked old-fashioned in the black-and-white photograph, which made her two-piece suit look brown when it was, in fact, bright blue. They were picture-perfect happy, and their smiles blessed our house.

Could it be that things were other than they appeared? Could it be that Ma chose not to wear white because she wasn't a virgin bride? Could it be the bouquet in her hand was well positioned to hide her bump? Ma always said Da chose the date because it was the start of the tax year and meant he got the full twelve-month rebate for being a married man. That story had a ring to it. It may have been a convenient smokescreen, however, to hide the real truth. With their firstborn, Seamus (Shea), coming on February 5, 1949, they had to give themselves at least nine months for legitimacy. April 5 gave them ten months, and it seemed almost too perfect when I thought about it. I still couldn't broach the subject with Ma, though.

Thinking about it brought me to the circumstances of my own marriage. It was ironic that Rossa, my eldest born, came into the world seven months after Sheila and I married. We could have lied and said it was a premature birth. However, we made no secret of the conception and, indeed, we celebrated the news when it came. We told both sets of parents and brought forward our wedding plans. Ma had warned me I'd "get that girl into trouble" (how do they always know?), but she was absolutely fine about the wedding. Da, on the other hand, got very peculiar. He wanted Sheila and me to get married but not to live together after the ceremony. In his plan, I would continue to live at home, and Sheila with her parents. Neither of us understood the logic of this and dismissed it out of hand. He was furious at not being taken seriously. In protest, he refused to sign the wedding papers. As a nineteen-year-old, I was technically a minor and needed his signature to marry in a church. He relented at the last moment, and only after a furious row. It centered on clothes, of all things. He wanted me to get married in a suit that he would buy for me in a proper gents' outfitter's. I told him it would have to be black to match with what the best man and the groomsman were wearing. He accused me of trying to turn the wedding into a funeral by wearing black. He interpreted my attitude as a slight on his generosity and a rejection of his help. Nothing could have been further from the truth. It finally erupted at the kitchen table one night, and he threatened to hit me. Ma had to separate us. I told him I'd make my own decisions after that.

My marriage caused an upheaval in Da, for whatever reason. I knew he was concerned at how young I was. He was worried, too, that it might jeopardize my university career. I had just completed my first-year arts, and a degree was something he'd dreamed of me achieving. They were legitimate concerns, but why it had to end up in a row over a suit I'll never know. There were times it was just impossible to engage him in rational debate. He made up his own mind and, as if he were a stubborn goat, you either pulled his way or you fought him head to head. His postmarital plans for Sheila and me didn't correspond to any logic I understood, and I rejected them.

I never thought at the time my actions might have implications for how he saw his own marriage. Perhaps he was angry at my honesty about the pregnancy. Everything was out in the open, and Sheila still wore white. I felt under no pressure to get married. If anything, the pressure was in the opposite direction. It was part of the secular shift in Ireland that couples could now "live in sin" without the wrath of the church coming down on them. Da had lived through the era of no choice in the matter. The only alternative to the forced marriage was to get on a boat and leave. Some men married and still got on the boat—it was known as the "Irish divorce." My consent was freely given. Sheila and I had planned our wedding exactly as we'd wanted it. Perhaps Da felt otherwise. Perhaps there was a pressure he'd never articulated, and my circumstances had resurrected it for him. I certainly felt the brunt of his anger, and I didn't understand it at the time. After my day with Doris, I had good reason to believe he was angry, not with me, but with himself.

A short while after my trip to Blackburn, a letter from Doris came in the post. It was strange to see the familiar white envelope with the English stamp in the corner and the block writing with the word "Eire" at the bottom. On the back it was sealed with sticky tape.

Doris, of course, had learned her bitter lesson with the intercepted letter all those years before. After that she made sure her correspondence couldn't be steamed open. I studied the envelope over breakfast and wondered would the paper inside be the same, with her address printed in black italic in the top right-hand corner of each page. I wondered what her news would be. I feared she had discovered the broken table leg and was about to charge me with the destruction of a priceless family heirloom. I took a sharp knife and slit the envelope across the top. I withdrew the folded pages that were stuffed inside, and the phone rang. It was Ma at the other end. I felt like I'd been caught with my trousers down. I had a rush of déjà-vu that made me dizzy.

— I've just opened a letter from Doris, Ma, can you believe that?—I said.

— What does she want?—Ma inquired.

I opened out the folded pages and read the first sentence to myself.

Dear Peter, I never expected ever to start a letter to Dublin with those words again and it seems strange to be doing so now.

I hadn't told Ma I'd been over to England to see her. Now I felt like her secret lover in Da's absence.

— She's just wondering how we all are—I said—it's just small talk.

Ma was too excited to talk about Doris. She'd had a phone call from Australia that morning, and her sister, Dympna, was coming home. She'd been out there since 1952 and had married a Connemara man, Michael O'Toole. So Ma's sister and bridesmaid, Dympna Meegan, was coming home as Mrs. Michael

O'Toole, and what's more, she was coming home for good. She was bringing her husband with her, and they were going to buy a place in Ireland and retire. Ma was over the moon at the prospect of Dympna coming home. It was the first thing that had put the old excitement back into her voice since Da's death. She'd seen her sister and husband three years previously, when Da and herself made the trip to Australia and spent four weeks with them. But now she was coming home for good, and Ma had called me to say that something would have to be done with the spare room before they arrived.

I sat down with Doris's letter and read the opening sentence again. It was a simple statement of fact, tinged with profound sadness. It expressed her loss in a way that made her a child who'd been badly let down by Santa Claus. She talked a lot about her day visiting the grave and how the city had changed in her years away.

> *I find Dublin very different from the city I knew and loved. It used to feel like home to me, but now it doesn't. The streets are still the same but the magic has gone. I shall be back for Peter's anniversary on January 14, providing I am still capable of traveling. It was lovely to have you over here after so many years. Whenever you come to see Manchester play, there will always be a bed for you here.*
>
> *I've given a great deal of thought to what you said about your father and yourself. I think you are using the wrong word to describe him as a "womanizer." That is someone who has sex with many different women, and he had not that opportunity. Hearing the way you speak of him makes me regret I did not stay with him when he pleaded with me to do so. I am beginning to think we all would have been happier and he might still be alive today. My regards to all the Sheridan family. Doris.*

When Da died, it had been seventeen years since Doris had seen him in the flesh. I was glad to be able to speak lovingly of him and revive good memories for her. I had told her he was a "womanizer" because he was an incurable flirt, a character trait he passed on to all his male children, myself included. There was nothing new in that. It may have been hard for Doris to accept she was not the only object of his desires after Ma. Or maybe she was the only serious alternative, in truth. He had ample opportunity to visit her in Blackburn on his many trips to England for football and horse racing. His choice not to was deliberate, in my opinion, and it didn't tally with the sentiments in Doris's letter. I looked forward to clarification at our next encounter.

As soon as she came out through the glass doors in Dublin Airport, I recognized Dympna from the wedding photograph. She was plumper and older but undeniably Dympna. She had on a green cardigan and track-suit bottoms and a pair of Nike runners. She wore glasses that were flamboyant but too large for her face. Despite all that and over forty years away, she was a country woman from Knockbridge, just like Ma. It was strange to be meeting an aunt who'd left Ireland the year I was born. She looked overawed by the crowd. I put that down to jet lag. Michael was several years older than her, but he seemed much more present, more aware of what was going on around him. I greeted him in Irish, because Ma had told me he was from the Irish-speaking Connemara Gaeltacht. He returned my greeting, and there was a blas (accent) to his tongue that fifty years in Australia had done nothing to eradicate.

I noticed immediately they had no luggage and asked where it was. They told me a porter was looking after it. They wanted to get to the house and meet Ma. I was anxious to sort out their bags, but they were adamant that a man in a uniform, whom they'd met near the carousel, was going to bring everything to Ma's house by car. It was not a service I was familiar with, but they convinced me everything was being looked after. I brought them to the house, and there was much hugging and crying at the reunion of the sisters. Ma was holding herself together fine until Dympna made reference to Da.

— I can't believe Peter's gone, Anna—she said—I just can't believe it.

Ma broke down, and she and Dympna held each other in the hall while I brought Michael into the sitting room and offered him a drink. He gladly accepted the whiskey and raised his glass to the memory of Da.

— I gcuimhne d'athair. Ar dheis Dé go raibh a anam dílis—he said *

Ma and Dympna followed in after they'd cried themselves out in the hall. Within a few minutes, the laughter and the drink and the stories took over and banished the sadness. Dympna imposed her personality on the room as if she owned it. She was loud and confident, as befits someone who's survived in a foreign place. She had that sense about her of having shed her inhibitions. She was assertive and funny without being brash.

— Come on, pass that bottle, little one—she said to Ma.

— You go easy, big one, or you'll end up drunk—Ma replied.

Dympna looked over at me and winked.

— Is that any way for a little sister to talk to her big sister?—she said from behind a great big grin.

I'd never thought of Ma as anyone's baby sister before. She

---

*In memory of your father. May his soul be present at God's right hand.

was too much of a tornado to be a baby sister. She was only five foot one, but I never thought of her as little. It was hard to fathom a little tornado. Tornadoes are passionate. They are wild and destructive. That was Ma. With her older sister in the room she was "little one" again, and she wallowed in it like she'd been missing it all her life.

Dympna declared she had a present all the way from Australia. She asked Michael to get the brown suitcase, and he looked over at me like I had it tucked away somewhere. I reminded him of the porter who'd promised to deliver it to the house.

— Has it not arrived?—he asked.

— No, it hasn't come—I told him.

Dympna started to get boisterous at the news. She shouted at Michael.

— How much did you pay that little bastard?—she wanted to know.

Michael tried to calm her, but it only made her worse.

— I told you he was no good—she declared.—I knew he was no good, Anna.

Ma reassured her it would all be sorted out. Ten minutes on the phone and I established that the luggage was in lost property. I drove to the airport and collected the bags.

On my return, I found Dympna on her own in the sitting room. Michael was upstairs having a nap, and Ma was out at the shops.

— You're so like your father it's frightening—she said.

— Is that good or bad?—I asked.

— If you can't take a compliment, I won't give you one—she said firmly.

I had grown up with a vague image of Dympna. Australia— or Arsetralia, as Ma called it—was a long way away. I had no sense of what her life was like there, so she was a shadow in my world. She was only home a few hours and already I felt that we occupied the same space. Dympna expected things to be done for her. Already I'd been twice to the airport and back for her. I had no doubt the porter existed, it just turned out I was he. This was confirmed for me when she stuffed a five-dollar Aussie bill into my hand. I tried to desist, naturally.

— If you don't take that, I'll let the air out of your tires—she said.

— You would, would you?—I inquired.

— Don't ever doubt your Auntie Dympna, son.— She spat the words out like a cowboy spits out tobacco.

She brought out Ma's present to show me. It was a framed photograph taken in the botanical gardens with the caption "Peter and Anna, Melbourne, 1992."

— I took that photograph—Dympna said.

— It's lovely—I added—really lovely.

— Do you like the frame?—she asked.

— It's great—I said, and ran my finger along it.

— Don't tell Anna, it's not real gold—she whispered conspiratorially.

Dympna had arrived at a good time for Ma. It was obvious they got on, and I understood why Ma had chosen her as her bridesmaid. There was no doubting the mutual affection "big one" and "little one" had for one another. I was glad she was home in Ireland. I asked her about Ma and Da and where they met.

— They met in Dundalk Train Station, you know that, don't you?—she said.

The truth was I didn't know, but neither did it surprise me.

— Yes, I knew that—I lied.

— Anna swept Peter off his feet, did you know that?—she said.

I kept my mouth shut and let Dympna's question hang in the air. I slunk into the womb of the armchair and opened my ears to her words.

She was a legend in Dundalk. Everyone knew Anna. She had a supervisor and a manageress over her, but it was only ever known as Anna's Place. The men were mad after her. If you came in and ordered a cup of tea with a drop of milk and two sugars, you'd never have to repeat it again. She was afraid of no one and had an opinion on everything. She could fuck and blind with the best of them. Horse racing, football, it didn't matter to Anna. She loved Gordon Richards; do you remember him, he was a jockey? But mention Dick Francis and she'd go ballistic, she hated the ground that man walked on. I don't know why, maybe he'd let her down for a double or a treble. She loved the horses and knew the form better than most men. As for politics, if you got her going, you'd never shut her up. Anna could disband the Orange Order, get rid of the B Specials, blow up the border, and she could make cheese sand-wiches and a shepherd's pie while she was doing it. The local IRA boys used to come in and get her going. Gerry Kiernan used to smuggle guns all around Newry and Dundalk. He'd a terrible soft spot for Anna, but he was married. Not that being married ever stopped Dundalk men. They're whores for the sex, God forgive me. Cooley dogs are whores for barking, but the Dundalk men are worse for the sex. Gerry Kiernan used to say that if Anna could get charge of the Irish Army she'd march them across the border and unite the country in a week. He was right, too. You must remember that Anna did a lot of her growing up in Belfast. We were all dispersed because of what happened to Mammy. She died in childbirth on Anna. Daddy did his best for a few years, and we minded one another. Anna and me were very close, but we ended up being separated. Daddy couldn't keep us all together, he didn't have them skills, you see. Anna was sent to the Lower Ormeau Road in Belfast, to Minnie Kiernan, a cousin of ours. They were awful times. It was shootings and killings and burnings, the whole year round. It was a very bad time to be

Catholic. Anna never forgot it. She always said Belfast was a breeding ground for bigotry and there would never be any peace until the British left, or were forced out.

Growing up the way she did, she never had time to be a child. She grew up at twice the normal speed for a girl, and she was very grown up when she was twelve. Except to me, of course, because I could see through her. I could always see the "little one" in there. The men who came into the canteen didn't see that side of her. She was a wild woman, to them. She used to organize late-night poker sessions. Everyone brought something. I'd bring a bottle of whiskey. I was working in a hotel in the town, and it was easy for me to borrow the odd bottle or two. The card game wouldn't start until after the pubs closed. Only the privileged few got an invitation to play. Peter wasn't one of those. Anna liked him, but he was down the queue a bit. If Gerry Kiernan hadn't been married, Peter would have had no chance. Peter got tired of dropping hints and asked straight out could he come. Anna was as cute as a fox. She told him if he could offer something for the table it might help his chances. The next day, he presented her with a deck of cards. The box showed an ad for McArdles No. 1—an ale brewed locally in the town. When she opened the box and took the cards out, he'd scratched the word "McArdles" off the back of the first card and in its place he'd handwritten "ANNA." Then she flicked through the deck and realized he'd done the same to all fifty-two cards. He got an immediate invitation to the Friday-night game.

There were six playing that night. Four men and Anna and me. That's the way we liked it, two men apiece. I'm only joking, it was a serious card school, and we were more interested in the gambling and the money. Not that we didn't flirt, mind you, because flirting is a good strategy playing poker. Peter was intimidated at how good Anna was. I saw him trying to keep a serious face when she was smiling over at him. He tried to bluff a game with a pair of eights. Everyone backed down except Anna. She saw him with only a pair of tens and won the pot. Everyone turned on him—he was mortified. Anna leaned in and threw her arms around the pot. I saw him staring at her flesh and I knew he was having carnal thoughts.

— That's a better pair you're looking at than the ones you bet on—I said to him.

He went beetroot. I knew he was hooked, he couldn't take his eyes off her the whole night. From that on, he was in Anna's Place morning, noon, and night. They couldn't keep him out of there. He was caught in the canteen at times he was supposed to be working. His boss thought he was addicted to tea. A woman in the town, the solicitor's wife, Mrs. Lavery, missed her train to Drogheda because there was no ticket seller on duty. They hauled Peter in over it. He told them he had a sugar deficiency, and they asked him to take a medical. He refused. They transferred him to Athlone, and he refused to go. They threatened to sack him. No one had been sacked from the job in over twenty years. He demanded to be let stay in Dundalk. They refused. He wrote out his letter of resignation and showed it to Anna.

— What sort of an eejit are you?—she said to him.

Peter told her he'd applied for a job in Carroll's cigarette factory. It was just outside the town. Well, Anna liked cigarettes, no doubt about it, but she didn't like this. He had good years of service behind him, and he was going to throw it all away to walk into a factory job. He was only blessed she didn't have a teapot to hand or she'd have thrown it at him. He asked Anna what she thought of the letter, and she tore it up into little pieces right in front of him. I knew she'd marry him when she done that. He had been head over heels with her for months, but now I knew that Anna loved him, too. He'd grown on her. It was all those cups of tea, you see. People don't realize the magic powers that come from the leaves. It's dangerous stuff. You only have to look at China. Well, it happened in Dundalk, too. Peter didn't resign, of course. Anna made sure of that. They transferred him back to Dublin, and when they did, Anna resigned from the canteen. She didn't want to let him loose among all those fillies in Dublin. She knew what Peter was like, so she followed him. It was nothing to her to pack her bags and take flight. She'd been at it since she was a girl. She'd called many places home since she'd left Knockbridge. Belfast, Kilsaran, Drogheda, and Dundalk. Everywhere she'd gone, she'd made it her own place. She'd do the same in Dublin. I knew she'd make a family with Pe-

ter. She had the raw material, you see. She went there determined to make him her husband. And it's a good job for you she did!

Our peace was disturbed by a clattering from upstairs. It sounded like Michael pulling the bed out from the wall. Dympna was unfazed by it, which was odd. I wanted to kill him for the interruption, and at the same time I was concerned that something was amiss. I suggested I'd go up and have a look, but she dismissed it out of hand.

— He's only looking for a bottle behind the bed— she said.—I know all his tricks.

She winked at me like it was the most natural thing in the world. She took what was left of the bottle of whiskey from Ma's cabinet and went upstairs. I could hear raised voices, but Dympna's was the stronger.

— You're not at home now, you're in Anna's—she said.

— Tell me where you put the bottle, woman!—he demanded.

There was a sudden silence. The bedroom door closed, and the stairs sighed under Dympna coming down. She came back into the sitting room slightly exasperated, like she'd put a difficult child to sleep.

— He thinks he's in Australia—she said.

I nodded and smiled, but I was fearful for the future. Ma's world had been turned upside down by Da's sudden death. She had been so looking forward to having her sister home. It was too awful to think it might all turn to dust. Ma needed Dympna now, but she needed the Dympna that smiled down from the photograph on the wall.

— What happened when Anna followed him to Dublin?—I asked her.

It was strange calling her Anna.

— Did she marry Peter straight away?—I added.

They sounded young when I called them by their Christian names. They seemed foolish, too, running after each other, the way lovers do. Sheila flashed into my mind. Standing on Butt Bridge, the tears on her cheeks mixed with the rain. We'd had a row, and I'd run off, and she'd caught up with me as I crossed over the river. It was a stupid row, and we made up there and then. I wanted to make love to her, but what can you do in the middle of a rain shower? I grabbed her by the hand and we ran to the Project Arts Centre, in Lower Abbey Street. I was directing a show there, and we made love on a mattress that was part of the set. It may well have been where our firstborn, Rossa, was conceived.

Had it been as dramatic for Peter and Anna? I wondered. Did he have a secret train carriage he could bring her to when they'd had a row and needed to make up? Was it there they'd conceived Shea and decided to marry in a rush?

Anna got a job in Clery's Restaurant in O'Connell Street. The entrance was around the corner, in Sackville Street. In no time at all, she was running the place. That was just her day job, mind you. In the evening, she worked in the ballroom upstairs. They had dances six nights a week. Anna worked behind the bar, and that suited Peter down to the ground. Until Gerry Kiernan turned up from Dundalk one night. He was on the run from the Guards; they'd found some guns in a hay shed belonging to him. Worse than that for Peter, the wife had put him out, so he was, to all intents and purposes, a free man.

Anna was staying in digs in Dorset Street, and Peter walked her home one night and they met Gerry Kiernan going into a safe house in Frederick Street. That put the skids under Peter. "His Nibs" was too close for comfort. Peter suggested Anna move in with him, and she thought he was mad, because he was living at home. But if he was mad, he was pigheaded, too. He convinced his parents that Anna was throwing good money away paying for digs when they needed to save every penny to get married. They agreed to let Anna stay in the girls' room. She could have her own hall-door key, but there was to be no hanky-panky. They could live as man and wife after they were married, not before.

That's how Anna came to be a lodger in Friary Avenue. Peter's sisters, Lily, Anne, and Marie, adopted her. After a week, they didn't want her to marry Peter. They got free admission to Clery's dances, and they didn't want that to end. They'd never danced so much in all their lives. Peter was seeing less of her than when he worked in Dundalk Train Station. She was going to bed with his sisters when he was getting up for work. Not to mention that Gerry Kiernan was on the prowl. When Anna did have a night off, Peter's mother had her over in the church with the women's sodality. He knew he had to move. So he did what he always did in a tight corner, he gambled. He took their savings and went to Leopardstown Races. He had a tip for a horse, a sure thing, and he went to the track and gambled their life savings on it. The horse won, and Peter put a deposit on a house in Abercorn Road, in East Wall. I think it was number 12, a lovely little bungalow near the railway line, around the corner from St. Barnabas' Church. War broke out with Anna when he told her. What sort of marriage were they going to have if he made those decisions without her? He told her some story about losing the house if he didn't put the money down straight away.

— Well, what do you want to do—says Anna—lose the house or lose me?

I don't know what answer he gave her, but she packed her bags, left Friary Avenue, and arrived back in Dundalk to stay with me. I was living in a cupboard in the Imperial Hotel at the time. I told her she was mad. Anna was having none of it. It was her money, too, and he had no right to spend it without telling her. He had no right to gamble it in the first place. She was finished with him. All I could think was how much worse she'd have been had the horse lost. She was being stubborn, and that suited her down to the ground. It didn't suit me, because there was two of us living in a shoe box. I told her to bury the hatchet and go back. I thought she'd split my head open when I said it.

Between the jigs and the reels, Peter arrived in Dundalk. He'd managed to get most of the deposit back and said he was sorry. Anna was surprised, I knew by her. I could see the stubbornness melting away, bit by bit. He promised her it wouldn't happen again. He wasn't bluffing. I'd seen him bluff, and this wasn't it. I was so relieved when they made up and took the train back to Dublin.

Three days later, I had a letter from Anna asking me to be her bridesmaid. The pair of them were spending every spare minute looking for a place to live. Peter brought her to see the infamous house in Abercorn Road, and Anna fell for it at first sight. So they put a deposit down for a second time and secured it. Anna decided where things would go—where they would sleep; where the baby would go, God willing; where the sitting room was to be, and the kitchen, and so on. Peter got straight into the decorating, and he cycled to Abercorn Road every day after work. As soon as he tackled one problem, a worse one seemed to rear its head. The house turned into a building site. There were lots of nights he didn't make it back to Friary Avenue. He didn't even make it to Clery's for the last pint. By the time the wedding day came, he was ready for hospital, never mind a honeymoon. If you look at his wedding photograph, you can read his thoughts—Be the holy, I don't have to go down to that building site tonight—you can see him thinking it. The next day, they headed for boring old France, and I went back to my exotic shoe box in Dundalk.

Ma's familiar key in the door brought us quickly back to the present. She brushed her feet eight times on the rug in the hall and came into the sitting room.

— I've just been telling this buck all about you and Peter—Dympna said.

Ma looked over at me and cut me in half, quartered me, sliced me up like a smoked ham. Only Ma could do that to me.

The day she caught me in her bedroom with my hand under the mattress and I said I was looking for a sock. She knew I was lying. I was looking for a book Da had, *In Praise of Older Women,* and I figured she knew. It was written across my forehead. I still had to lie, but her look was worse than any punishment.

— What do you need to know that you can't ask me?—Ma said.

There were a million things I needed to know but could never ask. I was a parent. I knew all the stuff we keep from our children to protect them. It is so hard to let that shield down and reveal our true selves. I wanted to know about Gerry Kiernan and the late-night card games and the swearing and the gambling and Anna running away and Peter coming after her— I wanted to know them with all their failings. I wanted to know about Doris Johnson, too, and the real part she'd played in Peter and Anna's life. I wanted to lift that stone and look at what was underneath.

6

I decided to investigate the date of their marriage once and for all. My first port of call was Arran Quay Church. I took a taxi and got out at Smithfield, the great cobblestoned square on the low ground north of the Liffey. I was a snotty-nosed kid in this place, sitting at the front of my grandfather's horse and cart, pleading with him to let Nelly drink from the horse trough at the Queen Street end of the square. A chunk of the granite trough was still there, but it was a long time since any animal had drunk from it.

The thing I missed most about Smithfield was the smells that once competed here. The hops from the Guinness factory versus the malt from the Jameson distillery. The stench of dead horses from O'Keefe's knacker's yard against the hot gristle and fat of Donnelly's sausage factory. I could taste those smells, even though they were long gone.

I walked across the square among parked cars where animals had once been tethered. On the left, going up Friary Avenue, a row of red-bricked houses with gardens had replaced the Victorian dwellings that once stood there. My grandfather's house, complete with large double doors to let in the animals, had straddled the corner. It was in the cow shed he'd hidden guns seized from the Asgard ship out in Howth. It was in this house, too, that Peter, my father, was born. It was here that Anna came to lodge when she left the canteen in Dundalk Station and followed him to Dublin. From this address, 5a Friary Avenue, they were married in 1948. It was a house that didn't exist any more. In its place were four walls that contained new lives, making a new history, pushing itself out into the future to embrace a new city.

I walked down to Arran Quay Church and knelt in a pew at the back. I looked at the altar and heard the country and city echo of "I do" in my ears. I left the church and went around to the sacristy. I rang the bell. It seemed like a five-minute wait before I heard the bolt being pushed back and the lock being turned. A small white-haired priest of about ninety-five stood out from behind the door and stared up at me. His skin was the color of the Eucharist.

— Yes—he said in a most feeble voice.

I bent down to his level and did what you're not supposed to do in such circumstances, I shouted at him.

— I'm looking for the register of marriages for 1948.

The old priest reacted to my question like I'd activated a stomach ulcer.

— Not here, oh no, not here, wrong place—he said, and contorted himself—we're not a parish church, you're in the wrong place.

I could feel the bizarre workings of the Catholic Church in Ireland about to explode in my face.

— All our records are kept in Halston Street, that's the parish church. You'll find they have it there—he said.

Halston Street Church is a hidden gem that stands, literally, in the middle of the fruit market, giving it a plebeian feel. In order to get to it, you have to squelch your way through discarded oranges, apples, and bananas. The housekeeper who opened the door to me was cheerful and obliging, not the norm for that occupation. In a matter of minutes, I was standing in front of an enormous brown ledger with the words "Register of Marriages 1948" written on its front. I flicked through January and February and saw all the familiar Dublin names of the area—Walsh and Kennedy, Brady and Moore. The pages had become brittle with age, and it struck me that many of the people named here would now be deceased. Their children carried on their names and their traditions, of course. They worked in Guinness and the fruit market and what was left of the distillery. I wondered did any of them come back to pry, as I was doing. I flicked forward to the end of August and started to work backwards. If they'd lied about the date, the odds favored August or July. They were busy months in the register, with many recorded weddings. I worked my way slowly, meticulously from back to front. My finger stopped at the name Sheridan. My heart stopped, too. This was it. I looked for the Christian name. He was a Cornelius Sheridan with an address in Brunswick Street North, and the girl he married was Agnes Lacy.

I abandoned caution and went straight to April, found the pages for the 5th of the month. There, on the dotted line, was the unmistakable script of Peter J. Sheridan, a signature I'd seen so many times it was imprinted on my brain. Underneath it was Ma's hand, written as Anna Meegan, less familiar because I'd only ever seen it expressed as Anna Sheridan. The witnesses were recorded as Patrick Sheridan and Dympna Meegan, making the record as valid as it ever could be. I closed the book and looked at the front to make sure I wasn't dreaming. I rubbed my fingers across the numbers that were unmistakably 1948. I could feel the wedding party looking over my shoulder. I could hear my Uncle Paddy's unique laugh, the same that had filled so many Christmas nights in Friary Avenue, the laugh that had contagion running through it and infected us all, year after year.

— I'm not signing that book [small laugh], you're not going to get me to sign [bigger laugh], you don't expect me to sign my life away [hysterical laugh lasting several uninterrupted minutes].

I left Halston Street Sacristy and walked through the fruit market with renewed purpose. It was like I'd come out from under a dark cloud of my own creation and I was walking beneath an unexpected sun. I was never so delighted to be wrong about anything in my life. Da had stepped out from the past and confounded me. I felt chastened. I wanted to apologize to him for harboring negative thoughts about the circumstances of his marriage. I'd let those thoughts fester and grow inside my head. I'd replayed their marriage and reduced all their problems to a forced beginning. That was clearly a mistaken analysis. They'd married out of choice after a whirlwind romance. He'd left Dundalk and she'd followed and they married because they had to be together. I was exhilarated at what I'd discovered, but I was ashamed that I'd debased Da in my heart. I went back to Halston Street Church and knelt down.

Da, I haven't been able to reach you since you died, although I've been thinking loads about you. I'm sure you know that, from where you are. I've been thrashing around in your past, because I have to. There's something I have to learn, but I don't know what it is yet. You haven't given your permission for this search, but you haven't forbidden it, either. I met Doris, and I feel so sad about her, you were all she had, all she lived for, and she misses you so much it's painful. Ma misses you, too, of course, but at least she has us, her children, and it makes it that bit easier. I'm going to continue, and I hope I have your blessing, and I'm sorry for thinking the worst of you, and I'm glad I was wrong, I'm so glad I was wrong, I feel I owe you an apology, I'm sorry, amen.

I started a letter to Doris and tried to present my news as dispassionately as I could. No matter how I put the words down, I couldn't hide my delight. No matter how I expressed it, I pointed an accusatory finger at Doris. Yet she'd never directly said that Ma was pregnant on the wedding day. It was all inference and suggestion. It was my own suspicious mind that made the connections that now proved false. I was in no position to point a finger at anyone but myself. I tore up the letter and called her on the phone. She asked no questions, she just seemed happy that I was making her part of the family. She took every opportunity to call me by my name, she sang it out like her voice had just found it again, having lost it for half a lifetime.

— You're welcome here any time, Peter, my home is yours, and remember, Peter, you have a bed waiting for you if you need to stay over. I don't want you throwing your hard-earned money away on expensive hotels, do you hear me, Peter? You're such a spendthrift, I'll kill you, that's what I'll do. Are you listening, Peter? I won't kill you, you know that. I could never kill you, Peter. Never. Never kill you, Peter.

I was going to Blackburn to ask her why she had stayed loyal to Peter. Why had she remained faithful to a man she could never have? She hadn't seen him for the final seventeen years of his life, and she was coming to pay homage at his grave. She brought forty-seven red and white roses in remembrance of him. Why was she doing this for a man she'd never lived with? As I asked myself the question, the answer came. Peter was the father of her child. That was the link that united them. Amanda was my half-sister. For the first time, Doris made sense to me. She was related to him, and through him to me, and nothing could take that away from her.

I was sitting opposite Ma holding an emotional hand-grenade. I knew I had to pull the pin, and the only thing holding me back was the fact that she was in bad form. It seemed to be a permanent condition since Dympna and Michael had arrived home. On this occasion, however, it wasn't the returned émigrés but the previous night's bingo that was the cause of her upset. She cursed the number nineteen with such venom I thought it was a person.

— That bastard nineteen, I hate waiting on that bastard—she said—that's the third time in a fortnight he let me down.

When she calmed down over the fiasco at the bingo, I lobbed the question at her.

— Did it ever strike you that Amanda might be Da's?—I said.

Ma looked over at me with those steely, intelligent eyes of hers.

— Yes, it did—she said.

— Did he say anything to you?—I asked her.

— He never discussed it, no, but it did cross my mind—she said.

I was glad I'd asked, and the discussion was easier than I'd expected.

— It certainly explains why she's coming over to visit the grave—I said.

— That one doesn't need an excuse—Ma said.—If your father sneezed, that one was on the next boat.

It brought me back to the rows that erupted in Seville Place when Doris came to stay. I remembered the war over the sleeping arrangements, and how Amanda ended up sharing the double bed in Ita's room. Most of all I remembered Einstein.

— Do you remember Einstein, Ma?—I asked her.

She looked puzzled for a moment, and I could see she was thinking back. I could see it slowly dawning on her as she furled and unfurled her brow.

— That name rings a bell—she said.—What's this happened to him?

— You killed him, Ma, you flattened him with a brush.

Ma noticed the droppings first and left them undisturbed until Da examined them closely, turning them over to view them from all angles. He thought they might be the work of a large mouse.

— They're rat droppings, Da.—Ma wasn't going to be contradicted.

Da didn't want to get into an argument he knew he wouldn't win. Instead, he sent me out to the garage to get the traps. I knew what was on every shelf of Da's Aladdin's cave. I brought in the biscuit tin marked "Misc" and helped him fish out the traps that were in working order. He made a couple of adjustments to the springs with the pliers, and I got the rasher of bacon and cut up the rind for the bait. Da never used cheese, because, he said, there was no scientific evidence that mice liked dairy produce. According to him, they were carnivores, like man, and wanted to live in houses.

— They're no fools, they like their meat and their comfort—he said.

He put the rasher rind on the hook in the center of the wooden trap, and he let me light the match. I held the flame under the meat until it went crisp. I loved the smell of burnt pig. If the mice were anything like the people in our house, they'd come running for their grub. Da gingerly placed the three traps on the floor of the scullery, where the droppings had been. He went about his business and left the traps to do their work. At nine o'clock the following morning, the trap inspection took place. All three traps were facedown on the ground, and the bait was gone.

— This rat's a genius.—Da's tone was deadly serious.

How could he remove the bait and not set the trap off, we all wanted to know.

— Because he's Einstein.

— Einstein!

We repeated the name back and forth, and it stuck. Da went all out to destroy him. In desperation, he reverted to cheese, and the following morning the trap yielded a slice of Einstein's tail.

— I hope Einstein dies fornicating, the bad bastard.

Ma said the house wasn't fit for visitors, and we knew that meant Doris. She was coming to stay with her daughter, Amanda. Ma didn't want them coming if we couldn't get rid of Einstein. It forced Da to undertake drastic measures. He'd said yes to Doris, and not even a rat as clever as Einstein was going to force him to break his promise.

He removed the cover in the center of the garage floor and revealed the drains below. There were three pipes meeting in a central chamber. All the waste and effluent passed through this point, and as a consequence, it was a rats' paradise.

— You're looking at Einstein's house there—he said to me.

This was his abode during the day. At night, he entered our house and embarked on food orgies. Da was going to launch an attack right at the heart of his lodgings. The plan was to cement in shards of broken glass, so that Einstein would rip himself to bits on his way to, or from, our house. I couldn't help feeling sorry for the poor rat when, out of nowhere, a ball of hair jumped out of the drain and ran up my leg. I screamed and brushed it away with my hand. It was Einstein. The little bastard ran out the garage door into the yard and disappeared into the mouth of the drainpipe. I hoped I would never see him again. He was disgusting and obscene. Had I not reacted so quickly he could have wriggled into my trousers and made droppings of my testicles. I wanted Einstein dead. I wanted him crushed. More than anything, I never wanted him to come in contact with my body ever again.

Da brought out a selection of old newspapers from the shelf in the kitchen. They were all opened on the racing page with the results meticulously recorded. He dipped the newspapers in a basin of water before he stuffed them into the opening at the bottom of the pipe. I asked him what he was doing.

— I'm making Einstein's funeral pyre—he said.

He handed me the box of matches and nodded towards the papers.

— Send the bastard to hell, go on.

I bent down and held the match against a corner of the newspaper. It burst into flames, and just as quickly the flames vanished again, before smoke started to billow all around the pipe. Da was delighted, because another of his inventions was clearly working. He looked towards the roof and saw the smoke pump out towards the sky. He rubbed his hands together with satisfaction. There was no way Einstein could survive inside this crucible of fire. I figured if the smoke didn't choke him the wasps would sting him to death. There were dozens of them buzzing around the roof. They were pouring out from the eaves in a stream of black and amber. What I thought were dozens turned into hundreds. They were falling backwards from the roof, and they were not happy. In fact, they were the most agitated-looking wasps I'd ever seen. There were thousands of them. They started to bombard Da's head in relays, like fighter planes. He tried to ward them off with his hands, but it was useless, there were simply too many of them.

— Get inside, son—he yelled at me.

We bashed our way to the safety of the kitchen and locked the door behind us with the top and bottom bolts. Da was relieved not to be stung. Ma was at the table polishing his shoes when Ita came bounding into the kitchen and wanted to know why so many wasps were coming in her bedroom window. At the same time, Frankie pointed at the kitchen window.

— Look, bees—he said, delighted with himself.

Da issued the command order, and we all disappeared up and down stairways closing every window in the house. When we'd finished, there was the awful sound of angry wasps bouncing off the glass trying to get in at us. We were a family under attack, and we closed ranks. We were hemmed in, coffined, but we were in it together, we were united like never before.

We sat at the kitchen window looking out at them. It was like looking out at snow falling, only snowflakes were gentle. They didn't throw themselves at the glass like demented apes. Snowflakes fell softly and didn't carry a sting, but they weren't as exciting as the wasps. The wasps were dangerous, and too many wasp stings could kill you. Snow was exciting, too, in its own way, but overall I preferred the wasps.

Outside was full of noise and inside was quiet, except for Da, who kept pacing up and down cursing his luck. Ma told him to take the weight off his feet, but he wouldn't. His biggest concern wasn't Einstein or the wasps, his biggest concern was getting to the dog track where he worked nights. As things stood, he risked death trying to make it to his bike. It was standing in the back yard, where the greatest concentration of wasps were. He went up the stairs to check out the war situation there. While he did, Ma put on her heavy coat and her Sunday hat. She pulled the veil of it down over her eyes and headed out the back door into the swarm of wasps. We were screaming at her to come back in, but she ignored us. Out in the yard, she pulled the papers from the pipe and stamped on the flames. She picked up the scrubbing brush and held it over the mouth of the pipe. A couple of seconds later, Einstein stepped out in a sort of a daze. Ma brought the brush down on his head and splattered him over the concrete. The brains of the genius rat were visible in the red pool of his blood. Ma swept Einstein into a pile. She got a shovel and scooped his remains into the bin. When she was finished, she calmly came back in and closed the door behind her. She went straight to the medicine cabinet, where she brought out a remedy for insect bites. She had two on her shoulder and one on her leg. Ita said she deserved the Nobel Prize for bravery, and we all agreed.

Da couldn't hide the fact that he was proud of her. He planted a kiss on her forehead. He unbuttoned her blouse and rubbed the cream into parts of her shoulder she'd missed herself. Ita made her a cup of tea, and Shea buttered her a slice of bread and put jam on it. Johnny got a basin of water and put it under her feet. Ma luxuriated in the attention. Frankie was the only one who wasn't happy. He sat by the window and cried, because the wasps were flying away and he wanted them to stay. Da explained to him that the wasps were gone because their queen had left. He stroked Ma's skin and smiled down at her.

— You can only have one queen in a nest—Da said with authority—one queen and one only. If the queen leaves, everyone leaves. That's nature, and you can't buck nature, son.

I hadn't seen his will, but Ma assured me that Amanda wasn't a beneficiary. They'd made a joint will not long before his death, so the details were fresh in her mind. They had argued over aspects of it, as was their wont. Ma couldn't understand why he was providing a hundred pounds for masses for the repose of his soul. She thought it was too late for masses after you were dead. Ma felt he should take out the insurance before the accident, rather than after it. Apart from that, they left each other everything, so that one of them would have the last laugh, depending on who went first. They both agreed that, irrespective of who predeceased whom (and Ma said she never wanted to hear the word "predeceased" again as long as she lived), Gerard would be left the house. As the only one still single, they wanted to make sure he had a roof over his head for the rest of his life. There was no mention of Amanda, and no mention of Doris. Da never raised their names in the context of the will.

I wondered would their letters contain anything relevant to Amanda's conception and birth. They could hardly conduct a forty-seven-year correspondence and not discuss something so personal. Ma didn't have a view, but, then again, she didn't have the letters. I'd helped her look for them after Da's death, but without success. I assumed he'd put them somewhere for safe keeping and it was only a question of looking in the right place. With that in mind, I began a trawl of the house from top to bottom.

I figured they wrote to each other five or six times a year, so that meant there were at least two hundred and thirty-five letters. That wasn't easy to hide away, not in a small house like theirs. Unless, of course, they weren't in the house but somewhere else. I was in the attic going through old boxes covered in dust when I had an idea. I came down the ladder and rang his solicitor—nothing personal of that nature had been lodged with him.

At my wits' end, I began to look in places a second time, as one does. I searched in drawers and cupboards, knowing they weren't there but hoping they would miraculously appear. I went through the shoe box of stuff that contained some personal items, among them a recruitment ad for the RAF from a newspaper dated March 1946. I also found a telegram in a musty brown envelope. I opened it out and it had his name printed in that typeface familiar to telegrams all over the world.

Dear Peter and Anna stop gave birth today stop mother and daughter doing fine stop thinking of you as always stop Doris stop.

It was dated September 1950, the month and year of Amanda's birth. Doris couldn't have been long out of labor when she telegrammed the news to Dublin. Was Peter the first man she thought of because he was the father? There was a compelling logic to it. I refolded the telegram, slipped it back into the envelope, and put it in my pocket. I went out to the kitchen, where Ma was getting the dinner ready for herself, Dympna, and Michael, a routine she'd established since their arrival. As on other days, Dympna and Michael took a pre-dinner walk that entailed a visit to the local pub on the Malahide Road. Nicely inebriated, they came home and reminisced about old times.

Ma was sick, sore, and tired of "the good old days." She'd had her fill of it. It was all right for a week or so, but the honeymoon was over, and she needed to move on to what was happening today and tomorrow. She didn't need to hear about the boat journey to Australia for the twenty-fifth time. There were only so many times she could nod her head and agree that the weather in Ireland was awful, and that the cost of living in Dublin was a scandal. Dympna didn't know how a person could socialize in Ireland. Michael got into an awful tizzy over the price of beer. What Ma wanted to know and was afraid to ask was how they were going to buy a home in Ireland when they were leaving so much money in the pub every day.

Besides having Dympna and Michael living under her roof, trying to cope without Da really had her off balance. At the end of the day, she had no one to share her fears with. Herself and Da enjoyed a drink together in the pub every night, and now she didn't even have that. More recently, Da had joined her at the bingo, and despite himself, he enjoyed it. Once he'd won that first full house and come home with a wad of notes in his pocket, he'd caught the numbers bug. Now it was back to bingo on her own again. For Ma, it was the curse of abandonment revisited, and she didn't want to deal with being on her own again. Her sister's return, initially, looked like it might help offset her loneliness, but in reality it was having a diametrically opposite effect. Dympna's presence with Michael only highlighted the fact that Ma was alone. She was minus Da, minus her companion, and she would never have him back in this life again.

— Are you missing Da?—I asked her.

She threw the onions on the pan and shielded her eyes from the splash, but she didn't answer me.

— How do you feel about Doris coming over and putting flowers on his grave?—I asked her.

— I feel like digging him up out of the ground and punching him in the chest—she said.

I was taken aback by her anger. The ferocity and the suddenness of it were hotter than the grease on the pan. Despite that, I felt she needed to talk about it. She needed to let it out.

— How would you feel if he turns out to be Amanda's father?—I asked.

She took three hot plates from the oven and spread them on the worktop. She started to spoon out the food, plate by plate—boiled potatoes, grilled pork chops and onions.

— You children have no idea what I had to put up with—she said—no idea in the whole wide world.

As she released her bitter words against Da, three loud knocks came to the hall door. I answered it, and the lunchtime revelers trundled in. They filled the house with their bonhomie, but it didn't rub off on Ma. I stayed and talked to Michael and Dympna, not out of any real interest in the exchange rate of the Australian dollar to the Irish punt, but because I was worried about Ma. She was angry, certainly, and I wasn't sure if it was directed at me, at Da, at her sister and her husband, or whether she was angry at the world because it seemed so full and she was so alone.

7

I decided to take the boat to see Doris. I went into the city center and purchased a ticket for the night sailing. I'd traveled to Liverpool dozens of times, but I'd never before bought a ticket. That was all down to Da, of course. As a railway man, he was entitled to free boat and rail travel within and between Ireland and the United Kingdom. We were among the privileged ones who traveled free. Throughout the 1950s and 1960s, the journey across the Irish Sea was as common for us as a ride on the 24 bus to the Phoenix Park. Most of the people who took the boat did so out of economic necessity. They went to work in the factories of industrial Britain, and for many of them it was a one-way ticket and they never came back.

In those days, the boat left from a point opposite the Liverpool Bar, on the North Wall. It was Da's local, and we always had a drink there before we got on the boat. I used to stand outside the pub and watch the cattle being herded on. In their excitement to board, they'd knock each other down in the scramble. I was fascinated when their feet went from under them and they slid around like mountains of jelly trying to get upright again. The squeals of the cattle men were as bad as the animals as they waved their arms and poked the heaving flesh with their long sticks. As a child, I thought the cattle were going on their holidays. I imagined they'd be let run around the fields over there, just like they did at home. I nearly got sick when Da told me they were going to England to be slaughtered.

The mothers and wives who lined the quay wall were not so deluded. They knew only too well what lay ahead. They wiped their eyes with their hankies, because their men weren't coming back. In the ship's bar on the way over, the men drank beer so they'd forget, and they sang songs so they'd remember. It was always a great place to be as a child, because the men would force money into your hand, just for luck.

— A little something to remember me by—they'd say.

By morning, they'd troop off the boat with sore heads and forget that they'd ever spoken to you.

It was more civilized now. Stepping onto the boat, you could be forgiven for thinking you were walking into the Gresham Hotel. Men in uniform greeted you. Bars, plural, were everywhere, and restaurants where a hostess brought you to your table were standard. Cattle were present, but only in the form of sirloin steak served rare, medium, or well done. The bars were strangely quiet, with not a singing emigrant to be seen. It was only when I stepped out on deck that the past caught up with me. I could feel the biting wind that comes off the Irish Sea, I could feel it in my face just like I was on the cattle boat of old.

My first memory of traveling to England was coming to see Manchester United play Shamrock Rovers in the European Cup. I was very grown up, almost seven, and I was making my first

pilgrimage to Old Trafford. At home we supported Drumcon-
dra Football Club—or Drums, as they were known to us. On
this occasion, I'd come to support Rovers, because they were a
Dublin team. I didn't know that I'd be reborn that night as a
Busby Babe. It was all thanks to Da that I became a Manchester
United supporter, an allegiance I've held on to all my life. I
would never forget the power I felt inside the stadium that
night, and how helpless I was to resist it. Fifty thousand people
cheering as one, and when I opened my mouth, how I possessed that power, too. It was Da who'd bestowed it on me. He
hadn't chosen Shea or Ita, Johnny or Frankie. He'd chosen me.
He'd offered me the gift, but in order to accept it I had to be-
tray Ma. It felt like a terrible price to pay when I was only six.

Da made the announcement shortly after Ma brought Frankie
home from the hospital: he was going to see Manchester
United play Shamrock Rovers in the European Cup.

— You hate Shamrock Rovers—Ma said in a calm
voice.

— I'll be supporting Manchester United, won't I?
he answered her.

— You're going to see Doris, that's why you're going
over there—Ma said.

— What if I do? There's no harm in seeing a person,
is there?—he said.

Ma had Frankie on her knee and was changing his nappy.
She didn't have to wet between his buttocks, because tears were
falling from her cheek onto his white arse. I hated Da for making her cry, we all did. Since she'd come home from hospital,
Ma had cried a lot, and it wasn't all because of Da. She cried for
no reason, which was odd, because babies made people happy.
Ita told us that some mothers couldn't stop crying when they'd

had a new baby, and that it could go on for months. Da said it was depression and we weren't to pay any attention to it and Ma would grow out of it quicker. The main thing for us was to be happy as usual.

It was hard to be happy when Ma was crying. As soon as she started, we'd find something to laugh about. I'd tickle Johnny, or Shea would read a joke from the *Our Boys* comic, or Ita would goo at Frankie and try and get him to make baby noises. It didn't work, so we tried to ignore her, which was impossible. You couldn't pretend Ma wasn't there, because Ma was at the center of everything. All you could do when the depression struck was to stay beside her and feel sad, or go out and play on the street.

Sometimes I wished he'd put his arms around her instead of reading the paper. It didn't do any good when he ignored her. Once or twice I went out, thinking he might do something, but I looked in through the kitchen window, and he sat where he was with his paper. It was inevitable, I suppose. They slept together for eight hours every night, which was a lot of time with your arms around someone. Why would you want to do it during the day when you did it so much at night? All the same, it was nice to be hugged when you banged your head or cut your knee. It was better medicine than a Band-Aid, having someone's arms around you. Da persisted with his "system" of ignoring her tears, but it did no good.

— Why don't you come with me to England?—he said.

— Abandon these children and feck off to England?—she said.—Up to my neck in nappies, and you want me to feck off?

— I only made a suggestion. I won't go, if that's what you want—he answered.

Ma shook the talcum powder on Frankie's arse, and it went all over the room in a snow shower.

— I won't stop you going to England, oh no, mister—she said—I won't have you hold that against me. I might not be here when you get back, that's all.

So he brought me instead of Ma, and I worried the whole time that she'd be gone when I got home and I might never see my brothers and sister again. I was afraid to ask Da, because I didn't want to spoil the trip and I didn't want him to get in a temper.

I couldn't believe the size of Old Trafford. It looked like a giant spaceship with the crowds milling about like ants, forming lines trying to get in. Everything in England was bigger than at home. All around us, hawkers were selling the red-and-white of Manchester United. Calendar photos of the team with the words BUSBY BABES printed underneath. They were shouting at the tops of their voices, but I couldn't understand them because of their funny accents.

Doris arrived, and when she saw us she broke into a little trot and threw her arms around Da. I was left looking at the boy who was holding her hand. He was about my age but taller than me. He tugged at Doris's sleeve and called her "Mummy."

— You've put on weight, Peter.—She was laughing as she poked his stomach.

— It took good money to put that there.—Da laughed back at her.

It was good to see him laughing, because he hadn't laughed much since Ma fell under the black cloud. All he did was cut off from her and listen to her cry. It wasn't his nature to be distant. His true self was balancing bottles on his head, dressing up at Christmas, and acting the eegit. I loved seeing him happy again.

I didn't like Doris. I didn't like her sucking up to him. Da was a person, not a lollipop, he didn't need to be licked. She kept pulling at his jumper and going on about his beer belly. She was giving out about his pouch as though he were a kangaroo.

— It took good porter to put that there—Da said.

Inside the grounds there were stands, where you sat, and terraces where the people stood shoulder to shoulder. We were squashed together in two seats, the four of us. I was on Da's knee, and the boy was on Doris's, only it wasn't a boy, it was a girl, Amanda. She wore boy's clothes, had a boy's hairstyle, and was tall for her age. With my head of blond curls, I looked like her baby sister.

When Manchester United appeared, something happened and I started to cry. I didn't know what was going on until Da pulled me up and held me in his arms. Everyone in the stand had stood up and covered me in darkness. I thought I'd fallen into a black hole. Now I was up in the air again, where I could see everything.

— Come on, the Reds—Amanda screamed.

I opened my mouth and screamed, too.

— Come on, the Reds—I said.

The noise passed right through my body, and I felt part of the crowd. Up until then, I'd been a Drums supporter, like Da. Now I became a part of something English, a part of something much bigger than Ireland, a part of something that was like the church. Doris never stopped talking from the time the ball was kicked off. A hundred questions, a thousand questions.

— Why is he allowed pick up the ball?—she inquired.

Da was blue in the face, but he smiled at her.

— Because he's the goalkeeper—he said.

— Cheeky bugger, isn't he?

She laughed at her own joke, and that made Da laugh, too.

When United scored for the third time, she shook her head in disbelief.

— I think the Red Shirts have five extra players on the pitch.

I counted the players, twice, and there were eleven on each side. I started to memorize the names. Pegg, Whelan, Taylor, Charlton, Byrne, Edwards, and Colman. They were Busby's Babes, and Matt Busby was their father, just like Da was mine. They carried his name, just like I carried Da's. He'd brought me to Old Trafford. I loved him for it. I loved him for giving me United.

I hated the way he let Doris link him walking down the street. She snuggled right up to him and pushed her head against his shoulder. There were millions of men in England, and she had to choose Da to snuggle up to. I hated him for letting her do it. We walked down the street, and Doris took us the long way round so she could point out Peter Street.

— They named that street after me—Da informed her.

She reprimanded him with a slap on the arm.

— You're ever so vain, you are. Where's your humility?—she said.

— I left it at home—he pronounced with pride.

What he had left at home was Ma. He'd left her at home with no one to snuggle up to. We passed by Balloon Street, and Da declared Manchester the city with the finest place names in the world. Inside the station, Da showed Amanda the broken-thumb trick while we waited on the Blackburn train. She was completely taken in by it. When he showed her how the trick worked, she did it thirty times in a row for him, until Da must have been sick and tired looking at it. She didn't seem to realize Da knew what the trick was. She didn't know how to behave, because she had no father and no brothers or sisters. Finally, the train came, and Amanda wouldn't board it until Da promised he'd come out to the house in Blackburn the following day.

Doris's house, with its yellow bricks, was like Friary Avenue from the outside. Inside, it was completely different. It felt like a house that was sick. It had fallen into a sleep before the war and never woken up again. The walls were bare—no photos, no pictures, no plates, no crucifixes, no Sacred Hearts, no Blessed Virgins, just plain wallpaper.

I didn't stay long inside. Amanda had a ball, and we went outside to play. She was a good footballer for a girl. None of the girls in Dublin knew how to kick a ball, but Amanda had a really hard shot. She took five penalties against me and scored three. Then she went in goal and I scored five out of five. She asked me what player I was. I hadn't a clue what she was talking about. Then she told me I had to pick a United player and pretend I was him. I picked Liam Whelan, because I knew he was from Dublin. Amanda picked Duncan Edwards. I dribbled the ball up to her and slid it between her legs.

— Whelan beats Edwards—I shouted.

Da and Doris came out to the door and watched us. Amanda ran after me and took her ball back. I looked over at Da, and he winked at me. Doris got cross with Amanda and ordered her to put the ball down and play. She did, and I let her do the same thing to me. I could tell she wasn't used to sharing. After the game we went back inside and looked at the fish in the bowl. It got really boring after a few minutes. Da showed them how to tune in Radio Éireann on the wireless, and Doris got so excited I thought she was going to lose her voice.

— Irish radio, we have Irish radio—she said.

Her father wasn't in the least bit impressed. I knew he didn't like Da. I was glad he was Amanda's grandfather and not mine. He never seemed to stop giving out, the whole time we were there. When it was time to go, Amanda grabbed Da by his jacket and wouldn't let him leave.

— Show me more tricks—she said—you have to show me more tricks.

Doris slapped her on the hand, a real hard one, and still she wouldn't let go. Da bent down to her and asked her would she like to come to Dublin for a holiday.

— If you behave, we'll go to Red Island in the summer—Doris said.

— No, I mean for you to come and stay with us. In 44—Da said.

That was the signal for Amanda to let go and throw her arms around Da's neck. When she was finished hugging Da, she let go and did the same to Doris. I slid in behind Da in case she tried to do the same to me. I held on to his trousers, and I wondered what he was going to say to Ma when we got home. I was trying to figure that out when the awful thought struck me Ma might not be there. She could be gone and I'd never see my family again.

Doris met the train, and we retraced the journey we'd made some months before. She snuggled up to me, and I was comfortable with it. There was a plate of corned-beef sandwiches ready and waiting on the table. After the rigors of the night crossing, I was in no position to be choosy. Doris wet the tea, and while she was fussing around I checked the leg of the table. It was still broken. No one had sat at it since my last visit. Living on her own, she had no reason to pull it out.

— How is Amanda?—I asked her.—Do you see much of her?

— Well, of course I do. She only lives the other side of Blackburn, you know.

I did know some basic facts. I knew she was married and had three children. Da was very possibly their grandfather. Just as he was a grandfather to my own children. I wanted to bring validity to all that, now that Da was gone. It was time for the secrecy of the past to be set free. It was time to acknowledge certain things.

— There's something I have to ask you, Doris—I said.

— You can ask me anything you like—she said.—If I can answer it, I will.

— Is Peter Amanda's father?—I asked, and could hardly believe I got the words out without choking on them. Doris immediately started to rock back and forth, and I wasn't sure if that was her way of saying yes or whether I'd upset her. Then I realized she was clucking away quietly to herself, like a hen on an egg.

— No, she's not Peter's child—she spoke the words softly—but he was more of a father to her than any man.

When I got back from Ireland, I just wanted to die. I couldn't believe he'd gone and married Anna behind my back. I went down to Conefrey's, it's a hardware store down the street here, and I picked out a bottle of weedkiller. I went to pay for it, and Mr. Conefrey asked me what I was doing buying such a thing when we didn't have a garden. I couldn't tell him it were to commit suicide.

— We have some weeds out our back yard—I said.

— You'll only need a small bottle for that—he said.

I put the large bottle back on the shelf and paid for the small one. All the way home I worried that there might not be enough in the small one to do the job. I was so annoyed I'd let him bully me. He were only a small man, and I'd let him walk all over me. Back home, I took out the bottle and stared at it. It were a picture of a nettle about to wilt. It showed the roots under the ground and the poison attacking them. I felt like I was looking at a picture of my life. I'd found love, and it were poisoned. I unscrewed the cap, and I almost passed out when I sniffed the fumes. Then this strange thing happened. I became totally calm. It was like peace descended and took over my whole body. I realized it wasn't a picture of my life on the label. My love hadn't been poisoned. Not by me and not by Peter. The poison was other people. The poison was coming from those who didn't want us to be together. I wrote to Peter and told him what had happened. He wrote back and said I must never do anything to endanger my own life. He asked me to swear an oath on it. If I made that promise, he would always stand by me. He would never let me down. He would never abandon me.

The truth was, he'd jilted me and I couldn't accept it. I sat in my room and wondered what I could do. I'd let him slip through my fingers, that was the painful part. My father was right, I was innocent and naïve. I was gullible into the bargain. How could I tell my father he was right? How could I say that everything he'd foretold had come true? I couldn't confide in him, and I couldn't talk to Celia or my mother. There was only one person in the world I could pour my heart out to, and that was the man who had so badly let me down.

They brought the police officer, Alex Whiteley, around to talk to me. I couldn't face the world. I felt like I was in a siege, but it wasn't my fault. He had to shout through the bedroom door to me. I had it locked. He were very nice to me, the things he said. I didn't want to come out, because it was nice having him say those things. He said it made him feel bad that he couldn't see my face, so I came out to please him, and he came around for Sunday dinner. It was the first time we made five settings at the table, and it was the first time I drank two glasses of sherry in front of my parents. Before the dinner was over, he'd been invited around again. My father was beaming that much, I thought he might be left that way.

The following Sunday was an even bigger success. After the sherry trifle, Alex took me out for a walk. The Victoria and District Brass Band were belting out a tune when he took my hand and held it. We went for a very long walk, and he never let my hand go once. He had a policeman's grip. We came back via Stenchall Lane, and at our back gate he bent down and kissed me on the lips. I have to admit he were a very good kisser.

I wrote to Peter and told him my news. He was very jealous. I was delighted. It were good to give him a dose of his own medicine. I liked to get him all upset. I even made stuff up to annoy him more. Then I found myself leading Alex on so I'd have stuff to write to Peter. I didn't really know what I was doing, because I didn't have a clue about sex. I had learned some basics in school, but I was very ignorant. I thought I couldn't get pregnant until after I was married. That's how innocent I was. In another way I must have known, because when it happened with Alex, the Sunday Mother and Father went out and left us on our own in the house, I took a hot bath thinking everything would just pour out of me. Well, I couldn't have been more wrong, because I got caught the very first time.

I thought my life was over when I got the news. I didn't care about my parents. I didn't care about the neighbors. What would I tell Peter? That's all that concerned me. I'd let myself down, and I knew he'd be disappointed. I knew Peter was married, but even then I always thought I'd save myself for him. I suspected he might not want to write to me ever again after the way I'd behaved. How wrong I was. He wrote to me, he wrote letter after letter, supporting me in my condition. He didn't judge me, he just offered his support. I thought it would finish us, and I ended up loving him more. It caused terrible upset here. Celia said I'd brought shame on us, and my mother couldn't even look at me without tears of disappointment welling up in her eyes. My father went to the Crown and Anchor pub, and he drank four pints of Tetley's and two Scotch whiskies, and he had to be carried home unconscious. As far as he was concerned, the police were now the criminals. The rule of law and disorder, he called it. He wasn't going to take it sitting down, he said, when he was lying sprawled out on the floor. We were a legitimate family since the Magna Carta, and we had the certificates to prove it. Nothing was going to turn him into an illegitimate grandfather.

Alex asked me to marry him, but I wasn't sure. I didn't love him, you see. I agreed to a trial, and we moved in together. It were only a small place, but it were home. Alex went to work, and I minded Amanda. She was a very good baby, and there was very little minding on her. Everyone doted on her, especially Father. I could tell he wanted more grandchildren, and he dropped hints more than once about me getting married and settling down. One night Alex came home late and I were writing a letter. I didn't notice at first, but he had a few drinks taken. He'd been down at the Crown and Anchor with my dad. He asked me to put the pen down, and I asked him to give me a few minutes, and he got very obstreperous. He demanded I stop writing, and I said no. Then he asked me who I were writing to.

— I'm writing to Peter in Dublin—I said.

— That will all have to stop after we're married—he said.

— You'll have to think again—I said—because I'll never stop writing to Peter, not for you or any man

— You'll be obedient to your husband—he said.—That's the law of God and it's written in the Bible.

I never trusted men who quoted the Bible. I had a teacher in school who did that just before he used the cane. My father did it when he'd lost an argument. He always claimed he had God on his side. I didn't like a policeman do ing that. I especially didn't like him raising his voice the way he did. The next morning, when he went to work, I packed my bags and left. I came home with Amanda, and I finished my letter in peace and posted it to Dublin. Peter was the most important person in my life, and Alex Whiteley wasn't going to take that away from me. Alex was Amanda's father, but that didn't mean he owned me. As it turned out, Peter became more and more of a father to Amanda as the years went by. He knew all the games that children loved, you see. He wrote pages and pages of things I could do with Amanda. Whatever he was doing with you lot in Dublin, I was doing the same in Blackburn. I remember when she was six months old and I put her sitting on my foot like she was in a saddle and I bounced her up and down.

Jip, jip, my little horsey.
Jip, jip again, sir.
How many miles to Dublin town?
Three score and ten, sir.

Will I get there by candlelight?
Yes, and back again, sir.

Well, the look on Amanda's face was a sight to behold. Once I'd started doing it, she wouldn't let me stop. I thought she was going to be sick. I wrote back to Peter and told him Amanda was going to grow up to be a jockey. He wrote out all the street rhymes of Dublin for me. He put the words down one side, and opposite them he wrote down the actions that went with them.

Round and round the garden	*Hold out Amanda's hand and make a*
Like a teddy bear.	*circle with your index finger.*
One step, two step,	*Make a big jump with your hand and*
And a tickly under there.	*tickle her under the arm.*

Amanda was growing up just like she was one of you. She was growing up in Blackburn, but she was a Dublin child. The one great disadvantage was we never saw Peter. That was very hard. It was hard on me and it was hard on Amanda. I so much wanted him to be a father to us I had a permanent pain in my chest with the longing. It was unlike anything I'd experienced in my life. I wanted him to be with me. I'd saved myself for him, really. The one thing I didn't want to do was break up his family. I didn't want to take him away from Anna. I didn't want to take him away from his children. Catholics married for life, and I envied them.

Peter wrote to me about the problems with Anna. I don't think she knew how to control him. He were a great big baby, you see, and he wanted his own way all the time. Anna herself was too pigheaded. She got too stubborn with him. The only way to handle Peter was to stroke his ego. If I'd been there I could have told her, but I was stuck here with Amanda. The worst thing was, she put him out of the marriage bed. I could have told her not to do that. That hurt his pride. Peter needed sex. That's the type of man he was, he was old-fashioned. He didn't like it when his pleasures were taken away. He had to have his drink and his horses, and he had to have his marital rights, too. When Anna put him out of the bed, he turned to me.

Nothing about Doris conformed to any understanding of human nature I possessed. She confounded expectation at every turn. I was humbled by the true story of Amanda's parentage. Doris had committed herself more completely to Peter than if she'd married him. She loved him from a distance, and that distance intensified her love. The fact that he wasn't available made him all the more desirable.

I wondered had they ever consummated the relationship. Perhaps they had wild liaisons whenever Peter visited England and Doris came to Dublin. Perhaps the relationship thrived on infrequent but passionate sex. There was no doubt that marital problems existed in the bedroom of 44. After our return from Old Trafford Ma put him out of the double bed. There was no row, but that night she left his pajamas on the single bed, and Frankie took his place.

Da was leading a celibate life and wasn't about to apologize for something he hadn't done. He was stubborn, like a real Irishman. He didn't care that flowers would melt her heart and heal the rift. He was proud to be full of pride. He could survive on it for years, he could survive long enough for Ma to see the error of her ways and make the first move in the game of reconciliation.

A plane crash in Germany helped to heal the rift. It was the day after Shea's ninth birthday, February 6, 1958, and we were eating leftover birthday cake when death stole in like a mist and poisoned the air in the kitchen. I had never seen Da cry before. I'd seen him choke back tears, but I'd never seen him let go. Ma stood up to him in the middle of the kitchen and put her arms around him, and he half tried to push her away, but she held on to him.

— Oh, Da; oh, Da; the Busby Babes—Ma spluttered the words out—the poor little Busby Babes.

The evening newspaper had a picture of plane wreckage and rescue workers and snow and ice and the name MUNICH in big black type. We searched through the words looking for the names of the dead. Duncan Edwards was the first name I recognized. I had imagined that I'd grow up to be just like him. Now he was on the seriously injured list. Where was he sitting on the plane when it crashed and broke his bones? Did he hear the Old Trafford roar as his body slipped to the ground? Would it save him now, when he needed it most?

We huddled around the radio for news and waited for miracles. By nine o'clock, half the team was gone. Tommy Taylor, Roger Byrne, David Pegg, Johnny Berry, Mark Jones, and our own Liam Whelan. All had perished in the snow at Munich Airport. We were in mourning for the Busby Babes. Even Ma, who hated Manchester United, seemed very affected by the tragedy. She coaxed Da to eat his tea, but it was a waste of time. At half past nine, she made Frankie's nighttime bottle. She put on his little pajamas and handed him straight to Da.

— Put him to bed for me—Ma asked him.
— I'm not up to it—Da pleaded.—Really, I'm not.
She plonked him in Da's lap.
— Tuck him into the single bed for me, go on.
The tone in her voice was young and inviting.
— Did you say the single bed?—he inquired.
— You heard right.—She smiled down at him.— Now, just do it!

Da bounded up the stairs and wasn't seen again. Ma put on lipstick in the scullery mirror and sprayed perfume on her neck before she followed him up the stairs. We stayed listening to the radio for more sad news, but we were thinking of Ma and Da and we were happy they were back together again. It took Ma to make something positive happen from the wreckage of the Munich air disaster.

Doris went into her bedroom and came out with a box of photographs. I'd asked her had she any of us taken in the old days. I remembered she had a black-box camera at a time when few people possessed them. I knew she'd taken photographs of us the summers she came to stay. She produced an old-fashioned album with a ribbon in the top right-hand corner and placed it on my knee. I opened it, and there was a photo of Da I'd never seen before. He looked only sixteen or seventeen. He had a smile, but he looked terribly self-conscious. He was a boy, really, and that was what made it so revealing. When I looked closely at it, I could see a pimple on the side of his face, by his mouth. He was waiflike, too. There was no hint of the porter belly that was to come.

— He was nineteen when that was taken—Doris informed me

I always thought his wedding photographs made him gaunt, but he was plump in them by comparison with this.

— That was the photograph he used when he applied to the RAF—she said.

It was only weeks previously I'd come across the newspaper ad amongst his stuff in the shoe box. It was a strange completion of the circle.

— You do know he tried to join?—she said.

I nodded, but I was only vaguely aware of it.

— They turned him down because of his height—Doris went on.—I think it was more to do with his background myself.

— You know he always lied about his height—I said.

I was going to add the bit about penis size, but I stopped myself in time. I turned the next page of the album as a diversion. It was blank. I turned over again, and another white page looked back at me. I flicked through, and it was entirely blank. There wasn't one other photograph. The only thing it held was the single photograph of Peter taken when he was nineteen.

— I was hoping we'd be able to fill it up—she said without a hint of self-pity.—Things don't always work out as you plan them.

It was the album of the life they never had. The blank pages of an unrequited love. Sitting there with the empty album on my knee, I was sorry Amanda wasn't his daughter. It would have been so much easier if she were.

Doris produced a wad of black-and-white photographs and handed them to me. They were so resonant of the period. She'd taken them in the summer of 1959, the first year she came to stay with us in 44. I looked at the photos and wondered why she hadn't placed them in the album. Perhaps they were too real, and the album was for the wedding that never happened.

There was one of me standing in the middle of Seville Place. I was wearing a sleeveless brown jumper with yellow stripes that I loved to distraction even though it was falling apart. On my feet were an oversized pair of Wellington boots that made me look like a country kid out digging potatoes. Why was I wearing Wellingtons in the middle of summer? I was being punished, certainly, but I was being made to smile.

There were several group shots taken at the back gate, and a very poignant one of Frankie and Amanda, with her looking at him with the protectiveness of a mother. It brought back to me how close they became that summer. A funny one of Ita and Amanda holding hands like they've just discovered they are sisters and never want to be parted ever again.

Most interesting of all the photos was one of Peter with Anna and Doris, he in the middle with an arm around each of them. In it, they looked completely at ease with each other and with life. Doris and Anna were wearing sleeveless summer dresses, each with a different floral pattern, which linked them and separated them at the same time. They were both standing close enough to him that you could see the curls of their hair touching off the side of his face. His smile was one that said "cock of the walk," his arms said, "what I have I hold," the chest sticking up and out to the world proclaiming that he could satisfy his mistress and his wife.

— Did you have a sexual relationship with Peter?— I asked her.

She looked at me from under that shock of white hair and started to giggle.

— You're as bad as your father for the probing—she said.

It was the first time she had evaded one of my questions.

— Did you ever sleep with him?—I asked her.

It was all in the photograph. They were two women who had come to an understanding. Two women who'd stopped fighting. Two women who'd shared the prize. I wanted Doris to confirm what the evidence told me. I wanted to hear it from her lips.

— I told you before, I could never do anything that would break up the family—she said.

— So you didn't have sex with him—I said.

She smiled as if in remembrance of something. Perhaps it was an intimate moment they shared in Seville Place or Blackburn or Red Island.

— You believe I slept with him, don't you?—she said.

I held up the photo, the moment of togetherness frozen in time, and showed it to her.

— You seem like a threesome—I said.

— Yes, we do—Doris added—because that's what Peter wanted. He wanted us to live together in harmony. That was his plan.

He had brought Doris and Amanda over on a trial to see how they would fit in. He'd always been a great supporter of the harem. If he could have chosen a time and place to live, it would have been San Francisco in the summer of love, 1968. He'd tried to make 1959 such a summer. He was a hippie at heart. He'd brought Doris and Anna together under the one roof to share his love. Was it possible to share two wives, two mothers, and two families? If the photo was to be believed, the experiment was an outstanding success. Yet the concept of Ma embracing a threesome was contrary to my remembrance of that summer. She may have been putting on a brave face to fool the world, because she was anything but happy at playing second fiddle to another woman, especially a woman she had welcomed into the bosom of the family.

Ma didn't like Da "acting the goat" with Doris. No one really knew what acting the goat was. It was a country expression for messing, only it carried a lot more weight the way Ma said it. Doris came back after a one-day trip to Skerries and invited Da to the annual dinner dance at the Red Island Holiday Camp. Never one to say no, Da immediately accepted, without consulting Ma. The following morning, Ma started refusing food. By dinnertime, it was an official hunger strike, and Da immediately began negotiations to get her off. He said he wouldn't go to the dress dance without her. Ma wasn't interested, the damage was done, and she wasn't going to have it said she stopped him doing anything, ever.

That night, she stayed at home when Da went down to the Liverpool Bar.

— Don't you go down with Peter every night?— Doris said.

Ma didn't like the insinuation that she was some sort of

alcoholic. Not from the woman who was trying to steal her husband.

— Why are you sat here when you could be sat in pub?—Doris wanted to know.

Ma wasn't sat anywhere. She was standing by the table, setting it for the supper. The noise of the cups crashing onto the saucers was like a train station. She retreated to the scullery to wet the tea.

— There's nowt as strange as folk!—Doris said, and sighed.

The atmosphere at the supper table was tense. Da sat in his chair and Ma poured out the tea. We all waited to see would she pour one out for herself. She put the teapot in the center of the table and went to bed without her supper. The following morning, Ma refused breakfast. She could take on a hunger strike because she had principles. She loved all the Irish martyrs— Wolfe Tone, Robert Emmet, O'Donovan Rossa, Terence Mc-Swiney, Thomas MacCurtain—and she could die a martyr, too, if she chose. It was all down to her.

Da broke the deadlock in dramatic fashion. He went out to Skerries on the train and procured a third ticket for the Red Island dinner dance. When he produced the ticket, Ma sat down and ate her dinner. Da was delighted with the thaw, but he was taken aback, as we all were, when Ma announced she would not be going to the dance. She said Skerries was too far and she'd be home too late. Over the next twenty-four hours, there were twenty-four excuses, until Da concluded she'd gone soft in the head because of the hunger strike. Finally, when she was backed into a corner and had no more excuses left, she told the truth— she had nothing to wear. Doris had brought a special dress from Blackburn for the occasion, and Ma couldn't go as a tramp. She had nothing to wear and no time to have anything made. We kept up such a barrage of pleading, she finally relented and agreed to go. The next day, she went up to Guiney's in North Earl Street and picked out the material for her dress. She hadn't worn a new one since the day she got married. Once she got over the scandalous price of green satin, she was delighted she'd made the decision to go.

When Friday came, there was excitement like never before in our house. Ma was upstairs having last-minute adjustments made to her dress, and Florrie Graham from the salon in Sheriff Street was on standby to give her hair a final going over. Da was in the scullery having a shave, and Ita was ironing his good white shirt and his tie. Doris was in the easy chair reading her book, *Great Catholic Mothers of Yesterday and Today*. She'd been ready for hours and was agitated that Ma and Da were going to keep her late. Doris didn't know that being late was a religion in our house, and it wasn't about to change for the Red Island dress dance.

Ma came down the stairs and into the kitchen. We were under strict instructions from Ita not to mess, and we didn't. There was to be no whistling and no cheering, and there wasn't. Ma came into the room, and I didn't recognize her. From her head to her toes she was different. Her wedding photograph was on the wall beside the clock. In it, Ma looked pretty beside Da, who was as skinny as a barber's pole, but she looked more beautiful in the flesh. Doris was very flat-chested by comparison. Despite this, they looked like sisters. Da came in from the scullery mopping his face. His eyes were on stalks looking at Ma.

— You look beautiful, Ma—he said from behind a trance.

He turned his gaze to Doris.

— You both look beautiful—he said.

Gradually, we all realized why they looked like sisters.

They were wearing the same dress. They both had satin dresses that were green with two tiny straps that revealed bare shoulders. Doris had brought hers from Blackburn, and Ma had chosen hers in Guiney's of Dublin.

— I must say you have great taste, Anna—Doris said.

— You'll be the belles of the ball, come on—Da said.

They headed off, separated and tied together by Da, one on either arm, in dresses that made them sisters, green satin and bare shoulders, for one night at least, sisters on the same team, captained by Da.

In the days that followed, Doris couldn't do enough for Ma, and Da was like the king of Persia. He had brought the two women into his life, and he couldn't contain his delight at the way they were pulling together. He had gone against his own rules and made queens of both of them, and they in turn seemed happy to tend to his every need. He seemed more relaxed than ever before. He planted a kiss on Ma's lips in the middle of the afternoon, with all of us watching. Ma was embarrassed, but she loved it. He taught Doris how to balance a bottle of Guinness on her head. He put his hands firmly on her waist to keep her steady, and she was smiling with such satisfaction she let the bottle fall, and the contents spilled all over the floor.

There was no doubt the love of two women was good for Da, and for the present, it seemed, it was good for them, too. Ma came in to the table and sat down. Da had a bottle of stout open in front of him. Only the dregs were left.

— Peter has something to say to you—Doris announced.

— What is it, Da?—she said.

— Where have you always wanted to go?—he asked her.

Ma always said she'd love to go to Lourdes when a miracle

was due. Failing Lourdes, she'd love to go to Knock, if Our Lady was to make an appearance. Doris came in from the scullery with the teapot and the plate of buttered bread.

— Tell her, Peter—she said.

She didn't understand Da's sense of drama. He was building up to the big moment. We'd seen it all before. He reached into his inside pocket for something, but before he could retrieve it, Doris blurted it out.

— He's taking you to Paris—she said—and I'm looking after the family.

We were delighted for Ma but disgusted with Doris. She'd stolen Da's limelight, and he couldn't say a thing, because she was a visitor. Ma tried to raise objections, but she was drowned out in a chorus of voices that said she must go, and the lure of Paris proved too much for her to resist.

Doris ran the house like a camp. Ma and Da were only gone five minutes when she had a list of duties posted on the inside of the kitchen door. I was in terror that she'd replace Ma. If I could stand up to her, then maybe she'd go back to Blackburn and leave us alone in Dublin. On the Wednesday night, I came in filthy from a five-a-side football match. My knees were scratched and my neck was caked, because there'd been a muck fight after the match. Worse than that, though, I'd worn my good shoes out to play, and they were all scuffed at the toe. I only did it because I thought I'd get her into trouble. As soon as she saw the damage, Doris pulled out the metal bath and told me to get undressed. We never had a bath on Wednesday. I told her I wasn't getting into it.

— I'm in charge now and you'll do as I say.—Her face was bright red.

— You're not my ma—I said, and she went redder still.

— Take off your ruddy clothes—she shouted at me.

I knew if I caved in it would be over for all of us. She went out to the scullery to get the soap and towel, and as soon as she did, I slipped out the back door and ran up Emerald Street into the playground. Three minutes later, I saw what looked like a vision coming around the corner. It was a woman with her skirt hitched up and her legs showing. They were pale legs, but they were moving at great speed. The woman looked like Doris. It was Doris! She was making her way towards me. I ran through the players and headed for the girls' playground. I climbed over the railings at the far end to make my escape. I looked back and saw that the game had come to a standstill. Everyone was watching the madwoman who was after me.

— Run, Shero, she's behind you—someone shouted.

— Go on, missus, you good thing—another voice roared out.

— Don't let her catch you or you're dead, Shero.— The words echoed around my ears. I started to run down Mayor Street and ducked into St. Laurence's Mansions. I ran through the flats and out onto Sheriff Street at the far side. I was determined to lose her. I heard the sound of running feet behind me. I thought my heart was going to burst. I ran into St. Brigid's Gardens, but Doris gobbled up the ground and swooped on me like a bird of prey. She hauled me home by the scruff of the neck. I got undressed without further protest. I knelt in the water and bent my head in defeat. She pushed my head down and got it wet. She squeezed the shampoo onto it and started to massage it in. She didn't speak a word, and neither did I. She handed me a towel to wipe the suds from my eyes. I started to let myself enjoy it. She was much gentler than Ma. Ma dug her nails in and didn't care about the knots in your hair. Doris wasn't so rough. Her hands were softer. I hated getting my hair washed, but now I was starting to enjoy it. Maybe it wouldn't be so bad to have two mothers. If I could only have one, I'd have to choose Ma. After my bath, she made me put on Wellingtons, and I didn't like it. I couldn't play football in Wellingtons, and there were no puddles to splash around in. Doris took two shillings from her purse and told me to buy a single of chips in Aldo's. I knew she was bribing me.

— Are the chips for me?—I asked with a sour puss.

— Yours to do with as you please—she said.

I took the money and headed out the door. I felt a bit of a traitor, but not much. At least I'd stood up to her. She was a bit nice, the way she washed hair, I had to admit that. She followed me out onto the street with the camera and told me to say "cheese." I felt the two shillings in my pocket and thought of chips drowning in vinegar while Doris turned the silver handle and took my picture.

Everyone shone like a new pin for the homecoming. We practiced standing in line for when Ma and Da came in the door. Under no circumstances were we to hold out our hands and ask what present we'd been bought. As soon as we heard the back door opening, we jumped into position. Ma and Da swept in, and they couldn't believe the welcome and they couldn't believe the house. Frankie broke rank, ran to Ma, and threw his arms around her, demanding to know what his present was. After that, we all relaxed. Within five minutes, the house was back to normal. I opened the jigsaw of Notre Dame Cathedral and started to make it on the table. Frankie asked me to swap it for the Notre Dame stick of rock he got, but it was full of snots from his nose. Johnny started to work on his Notre Dame coloring book. Ita and Amanda played with their Notre Dame dolls, and Shea put ink in his Notre Dame fountain pen.

I stayed at the jigsaw for hours, and Ma gave me a hand before the tiredness caught up with her and she went to bed. In the end it was left to me, Doris, and Da. My eyes were closing.

I knew if I left them on their own she'd tell him the story of what happened between us. I battled on to the bitter end. At half past twelve, Da finally told me to skedaddle. I traipsed up the stairs and left them to it. My only consolation was that they might have other things to talk about. Or maybe they'd get stuck in the jigsaw and finish it for me. Whatever they were going to do, it was in the lap of the gods. I could only go to bed and hope that it was all for the best.

I looked at this seventy-five-year-old woman and thought of her chasing me all around Sheriff Street and Seville Place. I had never encountered such determination before or since in my life. She would have run over hot coals to catch me that day. I could see that same steely determination in her forty years on.

I wondered how Da felt back then. Did he feel pursued by her? Did the act of being pursued make him feel needed? Did he encourage Doris's pursuit of him, because he hated the part of himself that pursued Anna? Da could never admit to being powerless over anything, and it was a large part of his rage against the world. He blamed Ma for everything from backing losers at the races to not getting promotion in the job. She was the ultimate Jonah in his life. When Ma wasn't there to absorb the blame, he pointed the finger at us, his children. There was always someone putting the mockers on him, and it was a tale of epic proportions.

Doris represented Da's escape route from this emotional turmoil. In his doomsday scenario, she was the one he would turn to. So he nurtured her and kept the pursuit alive. Luckily for him, she was patient. Most women would have demanded a commitment, but Doris settled for the smallest crumbs from his table.

I asked her again had they been intimate.

— Peter told me not to lock my bedroom door—she said.

Doris slept beside the bathroom. Amanda was supposed to share with her, but she ended up in Ita's room.

— I told Peter my bedroom door was never locked where he was concerned.

I was glad that she'd had something of him. She'd pursued him, and he'd finally done something to satisfy her passion.

I thought of Ma, too, and the price she had to pay for the trip to France. She had brought Doris under her roof and shared Da with her rival. I had no doubt she did that because the alternative was to put him out of the house and break up the family. It was a price she wasn't prepared to pay.

8

Ma had hit rock bottom with Dympna and Michael. It was evident things were not right from their first day home. What had started out as a problem was now a crisis. Ma had covered up for them in the belief that it was jet lag and once they had acclimatized things would settle down. Since their arrival, they had established a routine that consisted of a lunchtime visit to the pub, a teatime visit to the off-license, and every other day a visit to the bank to see had their Australian dollars found their way into their Irish bank account. They had sufficient funds for day-to-day expenses, but the transfer of money was crucial if they were to put a deposit down on a house. They had decided to buy something close to Ma, because they liked the area. They had identified a number of properties while they were out for their walks, but they hadn't made an offer on anything as of yet.

Things deteriorated dramatically when they stopped sleeping at night. Their habit was to go to bed immediately after tea, about seven o'clock. They had a drink before they went up, and Ma wouldn't see them until the following morning. That suited her fine, because it meant she could go to the bingo and have some time to herself. That's how it stood until they started getting up in the middle of the night.

One of them would go to the toilet, usually Michael, and then he'd come back to the bedroom and have a drink and start a conversation with Dympna. Neither of them seemed to be aware that Ma was trying to sleep in the room next to them. They made no attempt to keep their voices down, almost as if they were unaware that darkness meant it was the dead of night. Once or twice, Ma banged on the wall and told them to shush, but all they did was keep quiet for a minute before they started up again. The result of this was that Ma took to sleeping downstairs on the couch. She'd tried everything else—she'd spoken to them as a couple, she'd pleaded with Dympna as her sister, she'd confiscated their drink, she'd searched their room and hidden their bottles, all to no avail. On one occasion, after a 4 a.m. cup of tea and a read of the paper, she tiptoed up the stairs and into her room. As she pulled back the blankets to get into the bed, she saw Da lying there. It took her a moment to realize she wasn't dreaming, that there was a body in the bed and it was breathing. She went hysterical and started to scream. The man in the bed sat up, and it was Michael. He'd gone to the toilet and come back to the wrong room. It was a horrible experience. She couldn't get over it, and it was the straw that broke the camel's back.

Ma was adamant, she wanted Dympna and Michael out of the house. She couldn't get a night's sleep in her own home, and she couldn't take it any more. She was just getting used to life without Da, and Michael turns up in her bed. It was more than she could cope with.

Myself, Paul, and Johnny sat down with Dympna and Michael. We decided on a show of strength, because we didn't want them under any illusions as to the seriousness of the situation. We sent Ma into town, and we waited in the living room for them to return for their dinner. They arrived in the door and were surprised to see us. We asked them to sit down because we needed to talk.

— So you're the lynch mob—Michael said.

— We're not here to fight with you—I said.—We're here to try and help.

We sat with them, spelt out the ground rules of the house and how they'd been broken.

— There's no drinking in the bedrooms—Paul said.

— No roaming around the house in the middle of the night Johnny said. We can't have that.

— Of course you can't—Dympna said.—How could you?

It was all very civilized. Wide-eyed agreements and promises and head-nodding and tut-tutting and expressions of regret. In the heel of the hunt, we asked them what their plans were. Specifically we asked them what they'd done about a place to live.

— We're moving down to Connemara—Michael said.—That's our plan.

Dympna turned to him and raised her finger in admonition.

— I'm staying here—she said.—I'm staying with Anna.

In a flash, Michael stood up and stiffened with rage. He started foaming at the mouth, and he raised his hands as if he was about to strike out.

— We're going where we'll get a drink—he said.—
You can't deny a man his drink.

— You'll have nothing left for drink if you keep carrying on the way you are—Johnny said.

With that, Michael started to curse and swear in Gaelic,
and I tried to calm him down, but the words came in a torrent,
like he'd been saving them up since he left Ireland fifty years before. I did my best with my limited Gaelic, but he sneered at me
like I was a landlord trying to evict him. He kept going until his
mouth went dry and the words wouldn't come any more and he
needed a drink to wet his whistle, but he couldn't ask for one in
the circumstances, so he just dried up.

At that point, Dympna reached out and touched me on the
arm.

— We need help, Peter—she said.—We have no
money.

Her simple words brought sanity to the room.

— Are you bankrupt?—I asked her.

She stared at me without answering. I looked at Johnny and
Paul, and our collective hearts sank at the thought that they
were penniless with nowhere else to go.

That afternoon, we discovered the missing money. They
had been checking in at the wrong bank. It had been sitting in
an account in Fairview when they had been calling to a bank in
Marino. It was a happy end, temporarily, to a very unhappy
saga. I went from being a bête noire in their eyes to being an
undiscovered saint of the church. Their Australian dollars were
finally safe in Ireland. That was the good part. The bad part was
that their money wouldn't buy a house or an apartment anywhere in Dublin. Unfazed by the tiger economy, they set off
for Galway to give Ma a break and to begin the search for their
dream Irish home.

It was only when they were gone that Ma realized how much pressure she'd been living under. She hadn't known the benefits of a good night's sleep for months. She hadn't been able to walk freely around her own home without the fear of disturbing the drinking duo. She hadn't been able to use the bathroom in peace. Once they were on the train to Galway, she cleared out their room and filled a plastic bag with empty bottles. Every drink known to man was among the collection. It was hard to believe two elderly people could consume so much liquid and not die.

The clear-out gave Ma a new lease of life. She was on fire again, just like when we were kids and she took to redecorating the house. It was sleeves rolled up and arms to the pump. In that mood, she lived life on the run, like a guerrilla. Nothing got between her and her objective, she was pure energy and a joy to be around.

I figured the news that Amanda wasn't Da's child would add to her general good humor. She listened with interest while I recounted the story of Doris and Alex Whiteley and how she came to have his child.

— How did you learn all this?—Ma asked.—Did she write to you?

— I went over to see her—I said.

— You went over to England? To Blackburn?—Ma seemed surprised.

I thought I'd offended her. Perhaps I'd brought back a bad memory of Da for her. A memory of him heading off to England to see Doris.

— You be careful what you believe, Pete—she said.

She never called me Pete when she was in bad humor. She

only called me Pete when I was in the good books. I was on safe ground, thanks be to God.

— She's not a bad person—she said—but there's badness in her, if you know what I mean.

Her response to my news intrigued me. She was cautious in her acceptance, as if she was prepared to face a more unpalatable truth. Her reaction revealed a deep skepticism of anything Doris might say. I was reminded of the photograph Doris had shown me—the threesome at peace with the world and with each other. Ma's outward show of serenity may have been no more than a front. She may have been in turmoil inside, but she was determined not to present a martyred face to the world.

— How did you feel about Da having an affair with her?—I asked.

— He never admitted that, but I suspected, of course—she said.

— How did you feel about her sleeping under your roof?—I asked.

— I didn't feel good, but what could I do, put your father out?—Ma said.— How would I have survived? Still, I had to do something, and I did.

I decided to take in lodgers. You know how stubborn your father could be. I planted the idea, and within a few days he thought it was a master stroke. I encouraged him to put an ad in the newspaper. He started to compose it. He had a great way with words, I'll hand him that. I couldn't get him to sit down and eat his dinner. Every spare minute he had he was composing slogans and catchphrases. He was spending longer than ever in his toilet down the garage, and he wasn't studying form. He was writing out advertisements.

Welcome to the Costa del Seville Place in the heart of Dublin. Attractive lodgings at your fingertips.

Walk by the Liffey, swim in the canal, or take a trip on the
mystery train. The delights of Dublin for the overseas tourist.

I encouraged him, but he lost the run of himself. We weren't a holiday
camp like Red Island. We were looking for one or two lodgers, not thousands
of tourists. He was highlighting all the good points of the city. Naturally, he
was a Dublin man. I mentioned some of the bad points. You'd think I stuck a
dagger in him. He didn't talk to me for a week. I pointed out the cost to him.
That got home. He settled for a simple ad in the end.

Lodgings available. Center city location. Adjacent to RC church.
All modern conveniences. Phone 41966.

I sat Da down before the ad went in and put it to him face to face. I told
him I would cook for the lodgers, I'd wash for them, I'd make their beds, and
on Thursdays I would collect their money and put it in my purse. There
would be no discussion about how it was spent. I'd given up my right to a
wage packet the day I'd married, and now I was getting it back. I wasn't taking in lodgers to be an unpaid slave in my own home. I put it to him straight,
and he didn't bat an eyelid.

He couldn't believe it when I took in four. I felt sorry for them, you see.
They were all lovely bachelors, country lads, and I knew what they were
looking for. I knew I could provide for them. I could see the pound notes, too.
I have to admit they were attractive. I always liked the color of money. It always seemed nicer in my purse than in someone else's pocket.

Da took on the reorganization of the beds. He put his back into it and
pulled a disc. He tried to claim compensation.

— You'll have to take me on a holiday to France—says he.
I looked at him and smiled.

— I hope it stays fine for you—I said.

I was in no hurry to spend the money. I looked at all the things I could
do, and I took a delight in doing absolutely nothing. It nearly drove him
mad.

— I suppose you'll be buying a new suite of furniture—he said.

I left a dirty long pause.

— I might—says I—and then again I might not.

It went on for days and weeks. He suggested linoleum for the kitchen floor, a gramophone to play records on, a snooker table for the lodgers but I knew it was for himself, a new cistern for his toilet, and new doors for the garage. He made a hundred suggestions, but I wasn't opening my purse to any of them. He could stew in his own grease for a little while longer.

It was around March he asked where Doris and Amanda were going to sleep when they came over in the summer. I told him there was no room at the inn. Well, he nearly went off the rails. He didn't see it coming, you see, and that was what drove him mad. I put my hands in the air, I was innocent. I told him the lodgers were his idea. As far as I was concerned, they were one of his master strokes. Every available space in 44 was taken up. The only room that didn't have a bed in it was the kitchen, and that's where we had our meals. There was no room, and it was his doing. I suggested Red Island for Doris and Amanda, and it was like I'd suggested putting them in Auschwitz.

He suggested we convert the garage, and I smiled and nodded my head. I went out and inspected it with him. Father Ivers parked his car there. I couldn't see Doris sleeping next to a Volkswagen. Not to mention the roof that leaked and Da's toilet down the far end, which was a holy show. He said he'd find somewhere else in the Seville Place area. I was happy enough with that. At least she wasn't coming in under my roof and rubbing my eye in it. Da could find somewhere for her, and he could pay for it, too. I knew it wasn't what he'd planned. He wanted to share us, and us to share him. I wasn't having any of it, but I couldn't tell him that. I was afraid of him, to be honest. I was afraid to go against him. I thought he might kill me. So I filled the house up with lodgers to keep her out. And it worked, too, because Da loved the lodgers. It gave him someone to argue with when he came home from the pub. He had no intentions of putting them out. Didn't he solve half of the world's problems philosophizing with them. By the time he got through six months of lodgers, I didn't think there was anything left in the world to fix. Apart from

*where Doris and Amanda were going to stay. He went knocking at doors in
Seville Place. I didn't ask any questions, and I wasn't given any information.
I didn't care what he did, because I had the lodgers. I think that's what kept
him here, wondering how I'd spend the money. I wasn't giving in to him no
matter how many times he asked. I told him one time I might go on a cruise to
New Zealand. The next week, a letter arrived from the embassy detailing entry requirements. He'd written off to them and not told me, can you credit
that?*

*He found a suitable bed-and-breakfast in Talbot Street, and he wrote to
Doris, too. He sent her the details, and a telegram crossed with the news that
her father had died, God be good to him. He went over for the funeral, but she
canceled her visit to Dublin that summer. You know all that, because you
went with him to Blackburn, didn't you? He took you with him, am I right?*

He took Ita to England for the funeral. She and Amanda had
become like sisters, and as Doris wrote to Da, Amanda wrote to
Ita, and vice versa.

— He brought me to Old Trafford, Ma—I said—do
you not remember?

I could tell she did, and I could feel her antipathy towards
Manchester United in that moment. I found it thoroughly reassuring, and I never wanted it to change, despite my own allegiance. Recalling all their great teams down the years, none of
them had a defensive strategy that equaled Ma's. Her control of
the playing pitch was awesome. I could only marvel at how she
contained Da and Doris. She did that and protected her own
babes with the ferocity of a lioness. She did it with a guile that
not even Matt Busby possessed.

— You think Amanda could still be Da's child?—I
asked.

— Nothing would surprise me—she said.—I know
she wanted his baby, I know that for certain.

Ma reminded me that Doris wrote looking for a companion for Amanda. There was no beating about the bush, she asked him straight out could he help. Da read out the request from her letter and tried to laugh it off. Ma always pretended not to care when he read from her correspondence. Most of the time they were letters filled with mundane details of life as it was lived it in Blackburn, England. Most of it was taken up with stories of Amanda and how difficult it was bringing her up without a father to discipline her and set down the rules. The only time she got real family living was on her summer trips to Dublin, and it wasn't enough to last the year. Doris had reluctantly come to the conclusion that she needed a brother or a sister, that a major part of the problem was being an only child. To that end, she was turning to Peter as the only man she could broach the subject with. Ma told him that he could go over and make a baby with her, that she wouldn't stand in his way. If he did, though, he needn't come back to Dublin. He could stay in Blackburn and live out the rest of his life there. Ma was happy to issue the ultimatum, because she knew if he did go the lodgers' money would at least keep a roof over her head. She was now a woman of means, a fatally attractive proposition for someone of Da's disposition.

— What did you spend the money on?—I asked her.

The family lore had always been that the lodgers paid for our education.

— You must have splashed out on something—I said.

Ma was keeping tight-lipped on her former life of extravagance!

— You know well what I spent it on—she said.

All I could think of was the snooker table in the living room, and I knew it wasn't that.

— I could never say the word and I still can't—she said.

— What word, Ma?—I asked her.

— I know I'll say it wrong, I always do—she said.

I was intrigued, because I genuinely didn't know what she was talking about. Was it some secret, magical word from my childhood that I'd forgotten?

— Just say it, Ma—I pleaded.

She looked at me and took a breath.

— Perfect—she said.—That's wrong. It's not a Perfect, it's the other one.

The image of the first car we'd ever owned immediately sprang to mind. I could picture it in the garage next to Father Ivers's black Volkswagen.

— It's not a Perfect, what is it?—Ma pleaded with me.

I couldn't help laughing at the memory of it.

It's a Prefect, Ma, a Ford Prefect—I said.

— Why can I never say that word?—she said

Because you christened it a Ford Perfect, and it's a much better name altogether—I said—better by miles.

I went into Stafford's Garage, on the North Strand, and picked out the car I wanted. It was a Ford Perfect, a green one, because I liked green. I sat behind the wheel, and it felt really comfortable. I held the steering wheel and I looked out the window and I looked in the mirror, and it was just perfect. Tom Stafford handed me the keys and I didn't know what to do with them. He showed me the place where they went and I put them in. He told me to turn over the car. I thought he was losing his marbles. How would somebody of my size turn over a car?

— Turn over the engine—says he.

So I did. I started the engine and I sat there. I must have looked a right eegit. I turned to the poor man and I had to tell him I didn't know how to drive. So Da came around and took it home, and I needn't tell you he wasn't slow in taking charge of the car. The plan was, he'd teach me to drive, and he brought me to Dollymount Strand. I couldn't figure out the pedals. I was so nervous I didn't know my left from my right. Isn't that awful, not knowing which was which? I spluttered up and down the beach for a half an hour, and I was seasick. Eventually, I got the car going, but the pedal got stuck. I couldn't slow the car down. Da was screaming at me to brake, and I let the wheel go in a panic, and we ended up in the waves. The car started to sink. Luckily, the tide was going out, so at least we didn't drown. Da had to put his coat and his shirt under the wheels to get us out. He drove home half naked and swore he'd never give me another driving lesson as long as he lived. I lost interest in getting behind the wheel after that. Once I got my messages picked up at the new supermarket in Talbot Street every week, I was happy enough.

I nearly divorced him over the car. The Perfect came closer than Doris ever did to breaking up the marriage. One morning, I got up and I had nothing to brush my teeth with. My toothbrush was gone, and I couldn't figure out where I'd put it. At the dinner table, I asked had anyone seen it. Meek as a lamb, your father informs me that he's taken it for the car. He's used it to clean out dirty spark plugs, and he's found a little compartment for it beside the battery where it's housed.

— You couldn't have taken your own toothbrush—I said.

— Have you looked at mine?—he says.—There's no bristles left on it at all.

— So you took mine instead?—I said to him.

— If you feel that bad about it you can have it back——says he.

I politely declined. I wouldn't dare take back a toothbrush that now belonged to the car. Can you imagine a toothbrush after cleaning spark plugs? It went from bad to worse after that. The first year we got the car, I closed the house down for two weeks and we headed south. The five of you were in the back—Shea, Ita, you, Johnny, and Frankie—and I was in the front with Gerard on my knee. Outside Athy, the heavens opened, and Da flicked on the wipers. They moved across the windscreen in slow motion, just the once, and then they stopped. He had to pull over, it was impossible to drive in it. He lifted the bonnet and messed around with a few things, but it did no good. He cleaned some fuses with the toothbrush, same story. After ten minutes, he looked like he'd gone swimming in his clothes. The rain looked like it was down for the rest of the day, into the bargain. I offered him a nappy to dry himself, and he nearly bit the head off me. Ten seconds later, he'd changed his mind and took it. He transferred me into the back and put Shea in the front and made a human wiper out of him. I'll never forget it, Shea leaning out the passenger window and wiping the windscreen with a sodden nappy. Someone was holding on to his legs. I was sure we were all going to be killed. I couldn't look at him. All the way to Tramore, I looked at the ground and said the rosary. I know we all laugh about it now, but it wasn't funny for me. Your father could bring me right to the edge of despair without knowing it. Still, it got us to Tramore, back, wipers or no wipers.

Later that summer, Doris was due in Dublin. Da was collecting her off the boat, and he made me go with him. I'd wanted to stay at home, but I gave in, I don't know why. She came down the gangplank with Amanda, and I could see she was impressed by the car. She praised it until she could praise it no more. Da soaked it up like a good sponge. He loaded the suitcases, and we drove to Seville Place. The plan was to let Amanda stay with Ita for a few days and to drop Doris to the Skerries train. She'd booked Red Island because there was no room in Seville Place. I gave her a cup of tea, and she kept going on about the car.

— I believe he collects you from the supermarket in the car, you lucky thing—says she.

I said nothing. I waited for Da to say something, but he sang dumb.

— It's wonderful Peter has the car for you now—says she—you must be very pleased.

I couldn't take it, simple as that. I couldn't sit there and let her rabbit on. I was furious with Da.

— It's not Peter's car. It's a family car. I work, too, you know.

She finished her tea and asked Da to drop her at the train. He brushed her aside and took out the sherry. He was determined he was going to get his way. He made us clink glasses and declare our friendship. I had nothing

against this woman. I knew what Da's game plan was. At about half eight,
I reminded him of the train.

    — The last Skerries train went at eight-fifteen—says he.—
She'll have to stay the night.

He was about to reorganize the beds in the house, but I got in before him.

    — You'll have to run her out in the car—I said.

    — I don't know if I have enough juice—he said.

I took a ten-shilling note from my purse and put it on the table.

    — Do what other people do, buy some—I said.

He never had juice in the car. In all the years we had the Perfect, I don't
believe the fuel gauge ever went above empty. There was method in his mad-
ness, of course. He kept it like that in case someone asked him for a lift and he
could always plead the sixth amendment—I have no juice. I didn't care if he
had to push the car to Skerries, she wasn't staying in Seville Place. He drove
her out, and he took it easy, because he'd had a few drinks. It was nearly one
o'clock when he got back. I was still up. The house was very quiet. I was sit-
ting at the table having a cup of tea when he came in. He wanted to know
what was up.

    — We're going to have to talk, Da—I said to him.

He sat down opposite and opened a bottle of stout. I had nothing pre-
pared. I didn't know what I was going to say.

    — You'd be happier in England—I said.

I have no idea why it came out that way, but it did. I looked over at him,
and he was thinking. I could see he was thinking very hard.

    — You're going to have to choose, Da—I said.—I can't live
like this any more.

I knew what he wanted. He wanted both of us, that's what he'd wanted
all the years, it's what he'd prayed for, the two loves of his life to work together
in harmony. I was asking him to reject one of us, I knew that. I was prepared
for him to walk out the door and drive away. I had six good reasons to make
him stay, five boys and a girl, but they weren't good enough if he wanted to
be someplace else. He hated making choices. He much preferred "maybe" to
"yes" or "no." It was why he was such a bad gambler. As soon as he com-

mitted himself to a horse and it lost, he had ten good reasons why he should have backed the winner. With Doris and me, he wanted it both ways. I wanted peace. More than anything else in my life, I didn't want to live in the worry of tomorrow. I'd felt peace once, real peace, I mean. Sitting in Notre Dame Cathedral, something came over me, something I'd never experienced before. Maybe it was the Holy Spirit, I don't know. I felt contentment, real contentment. I think I forgave myself for Mammy. I was looking up at the stained-glass window, and the sun was streaming in, and I felt the light taking me over. I always believed I'd kicked Mammy to death in my rush to be born. But that's not how it was, it wasn't my fault, I'd been left alone to grow up because that's what God had chosen for me. I felt I'd been blessed with a new way of seeing that day in Notre Dame. I could have that peace back. It didn't matter if Da walked out on me, I'd survived losing Mammy and I would survive losing him.

— I'm giving you a choice, Da—I said.

He took a long slug from the Guinness bottle before he put it down. I could see remorse written all over his forehead.

— I'm sorry about the car—he said.— It was wrong of me not to tell her. It was very wrong of me.

I couldn't remember the last time he'd admitted to being wrong about something. The apology was welcome, of course, but the car wasn't the real issue, and I told him as much. In his heart he knew. He was also aware that he couldn't put off a decision forever. No, I wanted him to make it there and then.

— I'll wait until they go home—he said—and then I'll write.

— What are you going to say?—I asked him.

— I'll tell her not to come any more—he said.—I'll tell her it's all over.

I thought he should tell her face to face. I didn't think it was something to put in a letter. He was upset, I could see that, and I didn't want to push it any further. At the end of the day it had to be his decision, freely made, and I didn't want him ever to look back and say I pushed him to do it.

— It's your decision, Da—I said—it's whatever you want.

— Jesus, Mary, and holy St. Joseph, will you look at the time!

It was half past seven, and the Macushla bingo started at eight. Ma leapt from her chair, grabbed the nebulizer from under the television, plonked it in the center of the table, and plugged it in. She put the mask to her nose and pulled the elastic strip over her head. The gas started to rise up through the tube, and as it entered the mask she sucked it into her mouth and down to her lungs. At the same time, she trawled through her handbag for her makeup. She pulled out a compact, and with a sponge she started to apply the brown substance to the part of her face not covered by the mask. If ever an image said "bingo junkie," this was it.

Ma used the nebulizer three times a day. It was particularly necessary prior to bingo, as she was going to sit in a smoke-filled hall for the next two hours. When she was finished with the machine, she applied her lipstick at the same time as she put on her overcoat. I was standing two feet away from her, and I couldn't figure out how she was doing it. It was a feat of Houdini brilliance.

Outside the house, I opened the car and told her to get into the driver's seat.

— Come on, Ma—I said—I'm going to teach you how to drive.

For a split second she was about to rise to the challenge, but in the end discretion won the day. Or maybe it was the thought that she might miss a snowball in thirty-six calls. She sat in, pulled the seat belt across her chest, and held it in her hand. I have no idea what benefit she thought it was to hold the metal part in her fist. Maybe she held it and said a decade of the rosary, just for luck. I said nothing. I'd seen her do this so many times, and it summed up the reason I loved Ma so much. It made no sense and it made absolute sense, because when we arrived at our destination she'd be out the door of the car and into the Macushla before I had time to blink. There was no doubt, she was a true guerrilla who lived life on the run.

We drove along Fairview towards the North Strand.

— Did he ever write that letter to Doris?—I asked.

— What letter would that be?—she said.

— The one telling her not to come—I said.

— You know your father, he put it off and put it off—she said—and then Frankie took sick, and that changed everything.

I was sorry I'd asked the question, and yet it was lovely to hear his name on her lips. It was so seldom she spoke of him. It was hard even now, nearly thirty years after his death, not to feel the emotions well up at the mention of his name. I wanted to talk about him, and I was sorry I was having to drop her off. The last time I'd brought his name up in conversation was on the twentieth anniversary of his death, April 17, 1987. At the time, I suggested to Da that we have a mass in his memory and invite the extended family. I was particularly thinking of my own four children, who'd never marked his anniversary in a special way. Da obviously brought the request to Ma, because the following day she took me aside and told me she didn't need suggestions as to how Frankie was to be remembered. I never felt so cut down to size in all my life, and I never raised his name in conversation from that day out. I was so delighted it had now happened organically, and I was trying to think of ways to prolong it, when we reached our destination and Ma had the door open.

— You can drop me here at the lights—she said.

— Maybe Frankie will bring you luck tonight—I said.

— Maybe he will—she said.— Thanks for the lift, Pete.

She was gone before I had time to savor it, but I was glad we'd talked about Frankie without a smidgen of rancor. Instead of going home, I turned the car around and drove down Sheriff Street and Oriel Street into Seville Place. I drove by our old homestead, which was now a school for dropout kids. It had always been a school, with Da as master of the house. His teachings and philosophy resided in the walls of 44. I drove slowly up the street, past the McGuirks' old house on the corner of Oriel Street. That was where I was sent to fetch the relic of Matt Talbot. There was great devotion to the Dublin laborer around the North Wall. Mr. McGuirk had access to a piece of the coffin Matt Talbot was buried in. The relic was brought to Temple Street Children's Hospital, and we rubbed it on Frankie's fragile head. There were reports it had made a crippled man walk and helped a blind woman to see. It didn't make tumors disappear, at least not Frankie's. In the end, Da ordered the doctors to go in and cut out the growth. They were not successful. For three days he struggled on, and we got to say our goodbyes. Finally, on the afternoon of April 17, 1967, Frankie slipped from us and, as Ma put it, "he went home to God."

The news from Galway wasn't good. It was a Sunday evening when I got the phone call from Mrs. Dempsey. She ran a bed-and-breakfast establishment in the pretty village of Oughterard just outside Galway City. She was at the end of her tether with Dympna and Michael. She'd had them staying with her for three nights, and during that time six other guests had packed their bags and left. The litany of their wrongdoing was a replay of what had happened in Ma's—they were drinking in their bedroom, and their activity was keeping other guests from getting a night's sleep. They'd already been put out of two other guesthouses in Oughterard, and before that they'd been barred from one in Kilcullen and another in Moy. Mrs. Dempsey understood they had relatives in the county, but the only contact she had was my number in Dublin. She pleaded with me to come and collect them, as she couldn't put up with another night of their carry-on. In the end, Mrs. Dempsey agreed to drive them into Galway and put them on the eight o'clock train to Dublin. In the meantime, I contacted the Dublin-based members of the family. Ma went to stay in Paul's until we figured out what to do.

I collected them off the train, and despite the fact that they looked weather-beaten, they were full of the joys of life. Michael had two days' growth, and Dympna had the appearance of someone who would relish a bath. I asked them about their travels, and they had nothing but good things to report. People couldn't have been more friendly, they said, apart from one or two guesthouse owners. Michael had identified a cottage on the shores of Lough Corrib, and he'd made an offer to the estate agent. As soon as the offer was accepted, they'd be on the first train out of Dublin. They didn't want to impose on anyone, especially Anna, she'd been so good to them since their return. They only wished they could say the same about the other people of Oughterard and their bed-and-breakfast owners, in particular.

— Mrs. Dempsey didn't have to drive you into Galway—I said.

— She didn't have to put us out on the street, either—Michael replied.

— That's true, she didn't—Dympna chimed in for good measure.

Their grasp on reality was extremely tenuous. The cottage at Lough Corrib did exist, but a phone call to the estate agent revealed that it was four walls, a leaking roof, and little else. It wasn't suitable for a couple of their age and in their situation— it needed money and resources to make it habitable. I wondered what Michael's relatives made of all this. On investigation, I found that a row over the cottage had led to a major rupture between Michael and his nephew (himself a man of sixty with a sick wife), which ended up with the returned emigrants walking out to embrace the open road. The first thing they did on arriving at Ma's was to fish out a bottle from their luggage and help themselves to a drink. I suggested they put the bottle away for the night. Michael was as defiant as Samson in the temple. It stood out proud as the cheekbones on his face. Dympna looked over at me and laughed, just like a teenager.

— He's a holy terror, that's what he is.— She giggled and reached for her glass.

They were active alcoholics in an advanced stage of the disease. They desperately needed to stop drinking and they couldn't. They had blown their return home to Ireland with drink and, sadly, they couldn't see it. A room and a bed in Ma's would only provide a safety net that prevented them facing up to their problem. It was time for clear and decisive action.

Affordable nursing homes in Dublin were almost impossible to find. The result was long waiting lists when we needed an immediate placement. Through a priest friend of Paul's, we found a nursing home that would take them in. We established that they were both entitled to an old-age, noncontributory pension. All told, they could be looked after with only a small, annual contribution from their savings.

Armed with the facts, Ma, Johnny, and I met them in the sitting room of Carleton Road. We met them at 11 a.m., prior to their visit to the pub. The atmosphere was good. Dympna had prepared tea and sandwiches, and even Michael seemed sober and calm. We presented the case for the nursing home, and they listened and when we were finished, Ma was the first to speak.

— I'm not putting you out—she said.— This is for your own good.

Michael and Dympna couldn't praise Ma highly enough for her hospitality, and she was reassured by their kind words. It remained to be seen what way they'd bounce. Michael leaned forward in his chair and spoke softly to the room, like he was addressing children.

— We've been talking the whole thing over—he said.

— We haven't been talking about anything else— Dympna said.—That's as true as God, little one.

— We've come to a decision and we're not going back on it—he said.

They were going back down to the west. I could see the defiance in his eyes. They were going to live and die in the cottage with the leaking roof. My heart sank at the destruction that lay ahead.

— We're going back to Australia—he said.—That's what we've decided.

— You couldn't live here—Dympna added.—You'd want to be a millionaire.

At that point, Michael stood up and left the room. He came back in, momentarily, and in his hand he had what looked like a wad of paper. He put it on the arm of the settee.

— We've bought our airline tickets—he said.—We leave on Thursday.

Ma got upset. She was losing her sister again, just as she'd done in 1952. This time they were both in their seventies, and the chances of them meeting again in this life were as good as nonexistent. No matter how we tried to rationalize it, it was a solution tinged with deep sadness. The last thing Ma wanted was to see her sister leave Ireland again. Yet she wasn't prepared to share her home with their madness. Ma was absolutely clear on that, despite the shock of their imminent departure. Ma was a survivor, and even in her sadness, she placed great value on her sanity and the sanity of those around her.

When the day came, I packed their luggage and sat in the car with Michael while the sisters cried their farewells in the house. At the airport, I accompanied them to the desk and checked their baggage all the way through to Melbourne. A mini-crisis erupted when the check-in clerk informed them they were fifteen pounds over their allowance. While the duo discussed what items to leave behind, I paid the tariff and sent the bags on their way.

I hugged Michael awkwardly, and then I hugged Dympna, who didn't want to let me go.

— Look after your mammy—Dympna said.

— I will, of course—I replied.

— If you're ever in Melbourne, come and see us— Michael said.

I watched them walk away from me through the departure gates of Dublin Airport that strange Thursday morning. I figured I would never see them again.

9

Ma couldn't help herself. It was two days to the anniversary, and that meant two days to a visit by Doris. She couldn't have her arrive to an untidy grave. It would be a nightmare to have her making comments that it wasn't being looked after. In normal circumstances, Ma would do her clean-up on the 14th of January, the day itself, but as always where Doris was concerned, there was no normality. She came on the night sailing and went straight to the cemetery, arriving there before the gates opened at 8 a.m. It guaranteed she was the first to pay homage on the anniversary, and it meant any tidying up had to be done in the days preceding her visit.

It was an adventure to walk through Glasnevin Cemetery with Ma. She brought the place alive in her peculiar way. Once she recognized a name on a grave, a resurrection followed.

— He's one of the Dundalk McArdles, they lived out the Carrick Road, he was a fine-looking man, he married a girl called Minnie O'Boyle, a great friend of Dympna's she was.

I'm surprised he's not buried at home, he must have moved to Dublin. He worked in the cattle trade, he was an exporter, his trucks used to go down Seville Place, do you remember them, McArdles Cattle and Sheep?

It was a lesson to follow her around. Every ten yards she'd stop and point.

— He danced in Clery's ballroom—she'd say—but he never married.

It was funny to look at headstones and think of them dancing. Headstones dancing alone, and headstones dancing with each other. Shy headstones and outgoing ones. Drunk headstones and sober ones. Headstones standing to the front and headstones slinking behind. There were at least a hundred headstones in Glasnevin that danced in Clery's.

— He was a pint of stout, and she was a Scotch on the rocks.

It was heartening to think so many of the clientele were buried together. Ma had once called time on them.

— Come on, finish your drinks, it's gone the time.

She made it a living, breathing place, this ballroom of the dead. It was humbling, too, how much she remembered, when I could barely recall what I'd had for my dinner the previous day.

— That's Sergeant Billy McGrath, look, his son was in your class in O'Toole's, am I right, he served out in the Congo, I know his wife, Sally, from the bingo.

We hadn't made an inscription for Da, so Ma was inspecting the headstones with a purpose—she was looking for ideas. She didn't like quotations from songs, and particularly "Danny Boy," which seemed to be everywhere. She thought it was stupid to publicize what music a person liked when he was alive. She didn't like bits of prayers, for similar reasons. She wanted the headstone to say something about the person who was buried there. She thought an address was nice, or a reference to what his trade was.

William "Billy" Burke, a dedicated father and husband who served Arthur Guinness as a cooper for over 50 years

Ma loved the shiny black marble, which she thought was very modern. On the other hand, she didn't like graves with a photograph of the person behind a piece of glass. She thought it was too much like a passport application. Da was in heaven and he didn't need one.

We reached the grave after what felt like about a six-hour trek. There wasn't a lot to clean up, in reality. Some winter leaves and grit had accumulated in the corners. We bagged the gunge, and Ma took out the container of water and the cloth, and she cleaned the headstone and the surround. There was a little subsidence on the right-hand side, and I brought it back up level with the aid of a small shovel. We raked the white pebbles and got them to put their best side out.

It was strangely cathartic being alone in this place with Ma. I felt connected to her in a way that wasn't always possible in our ordinary lives. I was sorry there wasn't more dirt to clean away. I was disappointed we didn't have to work harder to bring a shine back to the headstone. I didn't want to finish what we were doing. It was only two years since Da's death, and we could talk freely about him, there was no barrier, visible or invisible, our conversation was without restraint. Frankie had died twenty-eight years earlier, and his death was an emotional minefield that separated us. The pain of it was still fresh, the wound still open. Ma had lost a son, and I had lost a brother. I don't know if you can compare losses. Hers was the greater, of course it was, but we had never shared it, we had borne it separately and alone. She had protected her grief, and I had done the same. I had tried to acknowledge hers and been slapped in the face for my trouble. Perhaps her burden was too great to be available for me. Twenty-eight years on, time had done nothing to heal the rift. That's why this time with her felt so precious. We were in Frankie's presence, and I didn't have to choke back the tears when I said his name. We were kneeling over him and cleaning his bed and polishing the letters of his name so that the world could read it better.

— You've done a great job on Frankie's name, Ma— I said.

— Yeah, it looks a lot better, doesn't it?—she said.

— Why did you put "Francis" rather than "Frankie"?— I asked her.

— They advised us to put his name as it appears on the birth cert—Ma said.—Do you think we should change it?

It was a new experience. Ma was talking about Frankie and I wasn't falling apart. She was asking my opinion on something to do with Frankie and I wasn't being overwhelmed. For twenty-eight years I'd carried him alive inside my heart because I was afraid to bury him. I had kept him alive because it felt like too much pain to put him in a hole in the ground. But that's where he was. I was standing over him and acknowledging it with Ma for the first time in my life.

— You and I know it's Frankie—I said—and that's all that matters.

Ma nodded her agreement and knelt down to pray. I followed suit. I closed my eyes. I didn't want to be anywhere else in the world. I was in the right place. The journey had brought me here, and I knew for the first time I was kneeling on the answer. I had been thrashing about in the past, and what I'd been looking for was in the grave beneath my feet.

———

Frankie's death tore our hearts out because it made no sense. The only explanation was that we'd done something wrong and were being punished. Ma blamed herself for entering him in the bonny-baby competition. Hour after hour, day after day, she pulled the photograph from the sideboard.

— There it is, there's the only mistake I ever made.

He was ten months old in the photograph, sitting in a baby chair, his two hands held aloft, the little fists clenched, a possible reaction to the click of the camera. Or maybe it was his way of saying "cheese." He had such peculiar ways of saying things, which made us all laugh.

— I saw a man a million times once—that was his best one.

Ma pulled the photograph from the drawer and showed it to every visitor who came into the house. She held it out for viewing, not the photograph but the reverse side of it. There she pointed to the entry form that was still glued to it— Evening Press Bonny Baby Competition. In her best handwriting opposite "name of baby" she'd written "Frankie" and beside it in parentheses she'd put "(Francis)." She'd spilled so many tears on it, the form had turned brown, just like the earth he now lay in.

— I knew not to enter him in that and still I did it— she said.

Her crucifixion was public. She humiliated herself in front of every stranger who came into the house, as if it was the only way she could pay for her sin. We all had a story that implicated us in his death.

Ita remembered how the makeshift gate at the bottom of the stairs had been left open only for Frankie to crawl up and then fall back, headfirst, to the landing below. It was a fall that created a black-and-blue jigsaw all over his face. It was Ita who picked him up after the fall, and when she told the story you sensed she blamed herself for not knowing that the gate was opened in the first place. If only she'd been vigilant that day, Frankie might still be with us.

Shea told the story of Frankie and the ice-cream cone. It was the summer we went to Tramore in the Ford Perfect. Shea bought two cones from one of those kiosks that dot the promenade there. He handed Frankie the cone, and when he went to lick it, he missed his mouth completely and hit himself in the eye. He missed his mouth four times with the cone. Shea reckoned now that the tumor was just beginning to do its awful work, the tumor that grew inside his head and finally took his life, the tumor that might have been treatable had he said something at the time.

For myself, there was the time I ran him out of the house when I was practicing with my new guitar. He jumped on a passing horse and cart and then fell off and was dragged along the ground, banging his head as he went. When I watched Frankie in his hospital bed, I prayed to have that moment back. According to the doctors, the tumor had been growing inside his brain for many years. The medical facts were no explanation for why Frankie had to die, because it made no sense. It was hard to watch the pain on Ma's and Da's faces, there was nothing to be said that could relieve the suffering, it was a feeling of utter hopelessness and despair.

Da took it the worst. His hair went white, but he didn't notice. The real trouble was inside his head. There was a tumor nestling there, it was a genetic thing, he'd passed it on to Frankie, and now it was returning to kill him. The X-rays revealed nothing, but the headaches got so bad he felt like his head was going to explode. We lived with the blinds permanently down and everyone walking on tiptoe. We all knew that to say his name was to induce pain. We all carried the knowledge and buried it within. We only had to look at Da to see the living proof. So we all played our parts in the conspiracy to stay silent.

There were days Da thought the tumor had an intelligence of its own and could hide from the camera. There were times he suspected that it didn't have a material existence, that it came from the soul and had something to do with his past sins. Perhaps he hadn't loved Ma enough, or the whole family, for that matter? Perhaps God was punishing him for Doris, for loving her when he'd promised his love to Ma at the altar. The God he prayed to didn't allow for that. He'd gone against the commandments, and Frankie's death was the price he had to pay for his sin. It was that knowledge which caused the headaches to come knocking on his skull. They confined him to the bedroom with the blinds pulled down and the damp facecloth on his forehead to calm the crucible that was his brain. For a while it was touch and go whether he'd make it back to our world or not.

In the end, Da rose from the bed to take up maintenance of the grave. He packed his canvas bag with tools, including a wire brush, a small shovel, a bottle of water, a trowel, and a chamois cloth. He drove to the cemetery at off-peak hours so as not to get caught up in the chaos of other funerals. He did his cleaning and maintenance work before he knelt down on the surround and said his prayers.

He tended the grave so as not to talk about who was in it. It was such a positive thing to keep it clean, to have the headstone gleaming, never to let flowers wither on it, always to have the pebbles with their good side out. Da looked after all the grave's needs, it became his responsibility, his baby. The trouble was, he couldn't talk about the baby who was in it. He couldn't talk to Ma, he couldn't talk to us, all he could talk about was the grave, he could talk about it ad nauseam. Despite the reminders of Frankie everywhere, his Wellies by the back door that no one touched, his school bag still in its place, these presences were powerful reminders that actually blocked us from talking about Frankie, because we had all learned to remember him in silence. We had to trust that time would heal what we couldn't heal by ourselves.

I remembered where I was standing the day we buried him.
            — Your mammy and daddy need you to be strong— they had said.
    So I did what I was told. I became a man that cruel April day. My remembrance of it was very clear. I could see the small brown coffin as it went into the hole in the ground, and my promise to Frankie that I would remember him every day of my life. I wouldn't cry, no, I'd just carry him within, I'd protect his memory in my own way, because I was grown up now.
    Kneeling at his graveside with Ma, I was a little boy again. I was fifteen years old and about to discover the sweet power of whiskey. For a long time that potion worked. For twenty-two years from the day of his funeral, I drank alcoholically. I drank to forget, even though I had made a vow to remember. In the end, the conflict almost tore me apart and I had to stop. The water of life turned to poison, and almost killed me. My spirit had been crushed and I had to find it again.
    I was kneeling at Da's grave, but I was remembering Frankie. The tears were trickling down my cheeks, and they were tears I should have shed a long time ago. There were times I had wished it was me in the coffin and not him. There were many days when it seemed an easier way out of the pain. But I wasn't responsible for Frankie's death. It was hard for me to accept that. I wasn't the cause of Ma and Da's pain. I had suppressed my own grief because I thought it would help theirs. I had a right to express my own pain, and I'd suppressed it because I thought I needed to be grown up.

I turned my head to Ma, and she looked back at me. I made no effort to stop the flow. I didn't try to wipe them away. I let them come. I was happy to let her see I was crying.

— Do you remember how you felt in Notre Dame?—I said.

— Yes, I was at peace that day—she said.

— That's how I feel about Frankie—I said.

She smiled over at me. I felt childish in an adult sort of way. I was so thankful that I wanted to pray, only I didn't know what prayer to say. I reached out and took her hand in mind. I opened my mouth and started to speak.

— God, grant me the serenity to accept the things I cannot change, courage to change the things I can, and wisdom to know the difference.

Ma repeated the words after me. It was like we were healing each other. When I stood up, I felt lighter and Ma looked smaller. I had a tingling in my shoulders like something had been lifted from me. I put my arm around Ma and pulled her close. There was no resistance.

Ma pointed to the bottom of the headstone.

— Da—she said—it has to say Da on it.

It was strange she always called him Da and he always called her Ma. They were words of definition—he did the Da things well, and she the Ma things. That's how she wanted him remembered, as a father, someone who'd stuck by his family through thick and thin.

— Down there at the bottom—she said—all by itself. I like that. Da.

We'd spent hours looking for ideas, and now Ma had come with her own design for a headstone. She wasn't borrowing from anyone, she was going to make her own unique contribution.

At the cemetery office, Ma made inquiries about the inscription. It would take several weeks to have it done. She was in no hurry, she was content now that she'd decided on the wording. The grave was in a fit condition to receive Doris, and that, too, made her happy. When we got back to Carleton Road, she started immediately on the Hoovering. She was like a woman possessed. I had to remind myself she was in her mid-seventies. I plugged out the Hoover and ordered her to use the nebulizer.

— You don't have to do this for Doris—I said.

— I can't have her coming into a dirty house—she replied.

— The house is not dirty, Ma, and you're not in a competition with her—I said.

The truth was, they were still competing for Da. Even in death, the struggle continued. There would be no letup until they were all dead and buried. That might be sooner than expected if Ma ignored her nebulizer. The hum of it filled the room. It was funny to talk to her through the plastic and the gas. It was like having a conversation with an astronaut—ground control to Major Tom.

— You don't have to be here for Doris—I said.

— I'm only doing what your father would want—she said.

— She upsets you, Ma, and Da wouldn't want that—I said.

— She saved your father's life after Frankie died—Ma said.—I can't deny her that.

It was an extraordinary admission. She looked so vulnerable sitting at the table sucking in the gas that prolonged her life. It seemed to be a day for reconciliation. Maybe she was in outer space, like Major Tom, and closer to God. I was certainly on a high after our trip to Glasnevin. I felt her hand reach out across the years and touch me. Was it the same hand reaching out to touch Doris?

She turned off the machine and sat back in her chair. A silence filled the room, and Ma started to speak.

She wrote about Frankie like he was still alive. Her letters were full of stories about things Frankie did. Like the time she minded you when we went to France. She loved to remember that, of course. The week she got to play mammy. She brought it up at every opportunity. The night she cooked pork pies for tea was one of her tales. She called you all in, and there was no sign of Frankie. So she kept it hot in the oven for him, and by eight o'clock he still hadn't shown up. At nine o'clock she called the police and reported him missing. She thought he'd been kidnapped, because not long before a child had been abducted in East Wall and was never seen again. She knew that, because I told her before we left. Just to keep her on her toes. By eleven o'clock that night, she was on her knees saying the rosary, even though she was a Protestant. At twelve o'clock, she went upstairs to look for a photograph of him to give to the police. She heard a noise coming from our room, and she went in to investigate. She pulled back the blankets, and there he was with his thumb in his mouth, fast asleep. He'd gone up to our bed at four in the afternoon and fallen asleep. I suppose he missed us. He was unconscious when Doris found him, and she couldn't waken him up. That was the tumor, more than likely.

She always referred to him as her little rascal. It drove Da insane. Frankie never appeared to be dead in her letters. He was always running around doing things. She never missed an opportunity to drag Frankie kicking and screaming into her letters. Or laughing and crying, for that matter. Whatever he was doing, he was alive.

— I can't stand her writing to me about Frankie—he said to me once.

That was the only comment he made. He took out a pen and paper, but he never wrote the letter telling her to stop. That was Da, he hated confrontation. He'd rather have her letters coming in the door than tell her to stop. Even though it was making the headaches worse. He'd rather it killed him first.

I read the Frankie letters when he was upstairs in bed lying down. I never let on, of course. I liked the stories she told. I found them very emotional. She wrote about him in the present tense. She hadn't seen him in his hospital bed, and she hadn't seen him buried. So he was still alive for her, I suppose. I couldn't talk to Da, because he got headaches at the mention of Frankie's name. I thought he was never coming down out of that bedroom. There were things I wanted to say to him, like what were we going to do with Frankie's things—his school bag and his Wellies and his green-and-white school cap. I was going through all this when a letter arrived from Doris, and the first thing she said was to send her a copy of the "In Memoriam" we'd placed in the newspaper.

That was the turning point for Da. I have no doubt about that. It was after he read that letter he started to fight the headaches. He stopped giving in to them the way he'd been doing. He took out his pad and started to compose an "In Memoriam." He wrote down the first sentence and called it out to me.

The parents, brothers, and sister of the late Francis Sheridan, 44 Seville Place, wish to thank sincerely all those who sympathized with them in their recent sad bereavement.

His way with words hadn't left him. He'd written the name "Francis" for the first time since Frankie's death. Once he started, he couldn't stop. It was like he'd woken up from a coma and he had to record everything that had happened while he'd been asleep. It had to be a full list of thank-yous. Anything less would be a denial of Frankie. He was proud of his son, and he was about to tell the world. He wrote it out in one continuous burst, and from the time he finished, he didn't want to change it. He asked me what I thought.

— You haven't lost your touch, Da—I said to him.

With that the floodgates opened. I put my arms around him. He wasn't crying for Frankie, I knew that. He was crying for himself, because he knew he was going to be all right. He'd been nursing a broken heart and it could have killed him. He'd been living with one foot in the grave. It had taken something to jolt him back to reality. That something was Doris's letter.

The "In Memoriam" turned out to be forty lines long. That was an ex-

pensive newspaper notice. I reminded him of the one he'd composed for the lodgers. He'd whittled it down from six lines to three. He'd cut out the bit about the Costa del Seville Place. He laughed at me; it was the first time he'd laughed in a long time.

— You could leave out the clergy, they wouldn't mind—I said.

He reminded me of the rent we got from Father Ivers for the Volkswagen in the garage. Confrontation again, you see, he just didn't like it.

— How could I face him if I left out the clergy?—he said.

— What he pays for the garage space wouldn't buy twenty cigarettes—I said.

He took it up and started to read over it. His handwriting was meticulous, as usual. Every word was perfectly formed. I couldn't believe he'd written it through a blinding headache. Not a full stop or a comma seemed out of place. It was perfect even if it was forty lines long. He reached into his top pocket and took out his pen. He scanned down the page with it, looking for words to take out. I caught hold of his hand and stopped him.

— Don't cut it, Da, it's perfect—I said.—Leave it exactly as it is.

Ma fished through her handbag while she was still attached to the nebulizer. She pulled out her purse and opened it. From the back of it, she pulled out a faded white envelope. On the front of it, in Da's inimitable hand, were the words "Frankie's Acknowledgment." I pulled the pages out, and it was the original handwritten version and a copy as it appeared in the newspaper. I read the opening sentence, and it was exactly as Ma had recalled it. It then went on:

> *To all who sent mass cards, wreaths, letters, and telegrams of sympathy, those who attended removal of the remains from the hospital and the Requiem Mass and funeral to Glasnevin Cemetery.*

A special word of thanks to the doctors, sisters, and nursing staff of Temple Street Children's Hospital; to the parish and clergy of St. Laurence O'Toole's Church, the Sisters of Charity, Seville Place, and the Sisters and pupils of Holy Faith Convent, Dominick Street. The Head Brother, his class Brother, Brothers, teachers, and pupils at St. Laurence O'Toole's CBS, the teachers and pupils of the girls' school, Seville Place, the Head Brother and Brothers of O'Connell's CBS, the Reverend Brother Franthom and altar boys.

Also to his grandmother, uncles, aunts, cousins, relatives, in-laws, and family friends, especially those who traveled long distances, to the Social Activities Committee and our very kind neighbors, who helped in so many ways. Thanks to the Area Manager, Area Sales Manager, and CIE offices and staffs at Connolly, Heuston, Sheriff Street, and North Wall locations; also to Central Room staff at Shelbourne Park and Sister Mulholland at Meath Hospital. Holy masses will be offered for their intentions.

It read like he had to name everyone or a curse would fall on him. He was superstitious at the best of times. At the worst of times, he was pathological. The remembrance of Frankie was his bridge back to normality. Doris had been the catalyst and Ma the protector. Where love was concerned, he was a child, just like Frankie in the bed sucking his thumb the day he'd gone missing. It was chaos all around while he retreated into infancy, oblivious to the consequences of his actions. Da had promised to deal with Doris before Frankie's death had so horribly intervened and immobilized him. He had decided, at Ma's urgings, to tell her not to come to Dublin any more. Could he still do that, knowing she'd plucked him from the jaws of death? Could he banish her when her letters had saved him?

It was the summer of 1968 when she next came to visit. I had good reason to remember it, because I was sent down to meet her off the boat. Da had run into mechanical trouble with the car, so he sent me on the 53a bus to the terminal. I was surprised to see her coming off the boat without Amanda. I waited with her for over an hour until Da arrived, covered in oil. He couldn't get the car started, so he'd abandoned it. Doris wasn't the least put out. She wanted to go to Glasnevin straight away and visit the grave. She didn't seem to care that it was four miles away. I was put on the 53a with the luggage, and the two of them set off down the East Wall Road on foot.

Ma didn't have a clear memory of it.

— You don't remember the car breaking down—I said.

— Do I ever remembering it starting?—she said.

— Me knocking on the door with the suitcases, and the two of us dragging them down to the kitchen?—I said.

Ma took about two seconds before the picture of that day came into focus for her. I could see it register on her face.

— That was the time she only stayed one night—Ma said.

Now it was my turn to look bewildered. I assumed she'd gone to stay in Red Island as usual. She normally booked it for a fortnight. Why would she come over and stay one day? Why would she bring such an amount of luggage if it was only a trip to visit the grave? It didn't make sense, and yet I had no reason to disbelieve Ma.

— She went back the next day—Ma said.—I remember it clearly.

It must have felt strange for Ma to know Da walked Doris to the site of Frankie's grave. Perhaps it was the price Da had to pay for the Frankie letters. Nonetheless, it was a strange form of intimacy. It must have upset Ma deep down, no matter what her public stance on it was. I certainly didn't want to bring it up on a day that had been so positive for me. I felt so warm towards her, I didn't want to say anything that would upset her peace of mind. I wanted to protect that feeling into the future. I thought of Doris's impending visit and wondered about the strain it would put on Ma.

— I can meet Doris and take her off for the day— I said.

I was surprised there wasn't an immediate objection.

— You don't have to be available—I added.—You could be in Cork visiting Ita.

She looked at me like a child who was about to ask for a big bar of chocolate.

— Do you think it would be OK to do that?—she said.

I arranged to meet Doris at Wynne's Hotel in Abbey Street. On my way there, I passed by the store that had once been the Metropole Cinema and ballroom. It was now Penney's. Like a lot of Dublin's unique architectural heritage, it fell to the developer's hammer. In its place was a modern concrete box with windows that added nothing to the character of O'Connell Street, the supposed showpiece boulevard of the capital city. As I approached it, I saw a figure in black standing in front of the building. It was Doris. She was looking up towards the roof as if she'd seen something there. It was her stillness that was so arresting. I stopped at Eason's Bookstore nearby and looked in the window so I could observe her without staring.

I nipped across to Wynne's Hotel. I stood on the footpath and waited. When she saw me, she broke into a little trot. She must have thought it unladylike, because she stopped herself just as quickly and resumed a normal walk. We embraced and entered Wynne's Hotel. Doris pointed to a table in the corner.

— That's where I sat with Peter after the pictures— she said.

The excitement in her voice was palpable. So we sat where they had sat all those years before.

— Do you remember the Metropole?—she asked me.

— I remember it well—I said.—I saw *Ben Hur* there, and *Dr. Zhivago*, too.

— It's a shame they pulled it down—she said.—I stood outside it and had a little cry just now. So much of Dublin is gone, don't you think?

The waitress arrived at our table, and I suggested a bowl of soup and a sandwich. Doris was adamant she wanted nothing but a cup of coffee. She explained how she'd had her flask of tea and corned beef sandwiches in Glasnevin. It was now something of a tradition with her, a ritual that celebrated their first encounter, in 1947. From the moment she arrived off the boat, her whole day was a re-enactment.

She walked ten miles to and from the graveyard on her day in Dublin. I didn't know any other seventy-five-year-old woman who would manage it. I was thirty years her junior and I couldn't imagine doing it straight after crossing the Irish Sea. I reminded her that the route she took came about strictly as the result of mechanical failure—namely, the breakdown of the Ford Perfect. She remembered that I'd come to meet her and that I'd taken her cases back to Seville Place with me.

— Why did you only stay a day?—I asked her.

She fumbled for her bag and didn't know what to do with it. She poured more coffee and milked it.

— I was wondering when you'd get around to that—she said.

I was very upset that summer, because Amanda had run away from home. I wanted her to come to Dublin, because she always came. You were a family to her, and she loved coming. She didn't have anything like that in Blackburn. I were at my wits' end, and Peter was the only one I could turn to. I wanted to talk, and Peter suggested we go to Glasnevin.

I couldn't believe the change in him. His face, his hair, his weight. He'd aged about twenty years, and he wasn't the man I knew. It was like he was walking in the shadow of death. Peter had always been so alive, and now he was just a skeleton. I told him Amanda had been seeing a boy and they'd gone off on his motorcycle and were sleeping in a tent at some music festival on the Isle of Wight. He told me not to worry and said a nursery rhyme.

— Leave them alone and they'll come home
Wagging their tails behind them.

His heart weren't in it. I asked him several times what was up, and he just shook his head and kept walking.

At Frankie's grave, I took out a little statuette and placed it on the pebbles. It had an inscription on it—Á La Grotte Bénie, J'Ai Prié Pour Vous. Peter was surprised I'd found such a relic in Blackburn, but I told him I'd had to go into Manchester to get it.

— I hope you'll do as much for me—he said.

I asked him what colors he liked, and when he said red and white I figured it was because of Manchester United. I told him I'd put red and white roses on his grave if he died before me. That cheered him up a little bit, and he laughed. I was deadly serious, and he didn't know it. I never break a promise I make, never. We knelt at the grave and said some prayers. I prayed for the little rascal under the clay, and I prayed for the big rascal beside me, who looked like death warmed up. Peter blessed himself and turned to me.

— I don't think you should come to Dublin any more—he said.

I thought he were joking, and I asked him what he meant.

— I don't think you should come to Dublin again—he repeated.

— Have you been threatened by the IRA?—I said.

He assured me it had nothing to do with that. I asked him had it to do
with me being English, and he denied it. I remembered my Uncle George,
who'd served as a Black and Tan. He'd met Peter once, and they didn't get on.
I thought it had something to do with Uncle George. Then it crossed my mind
that he was still upset at being turned down by the RAF and he was taking
it out on me. I didn't understand the why of it, I asked him over and over
again what the reason was.

— I don't think you should come any more—he said, and kept
on repeating it.

I knew then it was Anna. I knew Peter, and I knew he wanted to be with
me. For twenty years he'd denied himself when I knew he'd be happier with me.

— I know who's put you up to this—I said.—I'm not stupid.

— It has nothing to do with Anna—he said.—I'm asking you
not to come.

I felt so disgusted with myself. I'd given Peter my life, and he was tram-
pling all over it. I'd come to pay my respects at Frankie's grave, and I was being discarded like a bunch of withered flowers. I screamed at him to look at me.
He turned around, but he would only look at the ground near my feet. I
pleaded with him to come to England. It was the first time I'd ever done that.
It was the first time I'd asked him to leave his family. I could see him slipping
away, and I didn't want him to die.

— Please come to England with me—I said.

He looked up at me, he finally looked into my eyes, and he had to push
the words out; it was horrible.

— I can't—he said.

He didn't have the energy to strangle me, but that would have been
kinder. I don't know how long I stayed there, but in the end Peter suggested a
taxi back to Seville Place, and I told him to leave me alone. He put his hand
on my shoulder, and I screamed at him to stay away from me. I wanted to be
alone because I was alone. Amanda had left, and Peter was about to do the

same. I heard his footsteps on the path, and I was glad he was leaving. My heart had been ripped out, but I was still breathing. It was the strangest feeling I'd ever had. I wandered around the graveyard, I didn't know what I was doing, I was looking for sad headstones to read. I found the Daughters of Charity, and there was one name, Sister Juliana, died when she was twenty-four years old. The same age as me when I met Peter. I wondered did she die of a broken heart. Maybe she killed herself to be with God. I talked to her for ages. I was having a conversation with her, and she called me by my name. I heard it as clear as day. Then I realized it was Peter. He was calling out my name all over the graveyard. I hid in one of those contraptions they throw the dead flowers in. They're ugly, big cages the size of four coffins. I covered myself up, because I didn't want to be found. I don't know how long I was there, but I felt a hand come in and touch me. I felt it at the back of my neck. I was thinking it might squeeze the life out of me when I felt another hand under my legs. I was lifted out of the bed of dead flowers. Peter brushed me down. I was covered in leaves and twigs and bits of stems. We left the cemetery and took a taxi to Seville Place. I was too upset to get out of the car. Anna came out and asked me in for a cup of tea, but I declined. Peter brought out the suitcases, and we drove to Talbot Street and found a bed-and-breakfast. He stayed with me, I didn't ask him, he stayed with me of his own free will. I wasn't to know it was the last time we'd share a bed. I'd love to have tried for a baby that night, but I was on the pill. I always made sure I was on it before I came to Dublin. The next day, I pleaded with him again. He had to look after the family, he said.

— Do we have a future?—I asked him.

— Nobody knows what the future holds—he said.

We went to the North Wall and he put me on the boat. He banished me from Ireland. He sent me home, and I couldn't help thinking I'd never see him again. I hated the fact I was English. I hated being a Protestant, too. They were the things that kept us apart. I was going home to an empty country and an empty house. I was turning my back on the only thing I loved in the world. What sort of a future was that?

I was glad Doris had told me her story. I was equally glad to protect Ma from it. She didn't need to feel its bitterness.

Doris wouldn't hear of me paying for her coffee. She dived into her bag and pulled out her flask and her sailing tickets and three sticks of rock, which she put on the table. Finally, she found her purse hiding down the bottom, and she paid the waitress with a crisp Irish twenty-pound note.

— Are they for your grandchildren?—I inquired of the sticks of rock.

— Yes, they are, and you wouldn't believe the trouble I had laying my hands on them—she said.—I tried every shop from Glasnevin to here.

Did she marry the fella in the tent?—I inquired.

Doris looked at me like I'd asked her to take her clothes off.

— Whatever are you talking about?—she said

Her voice went up several octaves in her excitement.

— Amanda—I whispered—did she marry the fella in the tent?

It turned out she had done precisely that. Max Dryden, her husband, was a draftsman and a pillar of English society. All Doris's worry back then was for nothing, and Da's advice à la Little Bo Peep proved to be prophetic.

We left Wynne's Hotel, and I brought Doris back to my home so she could have a lie-down before the night sailing that lay ahead of her. I drove home via Seville Place, and she was very excited to see the old homestead. She couldn't believe that the house she'd once stayed in was now a school.

— Why did you use contraceptives when you slept with Peter?—I asked her.

— My, we're very forward today—she said.

— You don't have to answer if you don't want to—
I said.

— I never wanted to take Peter away from his family, and a baby might have done that—she said.—Catholics married for life, I knew that.

— But you wrote to Da looking for a companion for Amanda—I said.—At least that's what Ma remembers.

The words were no sooner out of my mouth than I wanted to bite my tongue off. The last thing I wanted to do was implicate Ma in a controversy regarding the past. I simply wanted to elicit Doris's story from her without contradicting it or making judgments on it. It was the first time I had crossed that boundary, and I was sure it might cause her to back off.

— I never wrote such a letter—Doris said.—I never asked Peter to give me a baby.

Doris had put down a clear marker that she was not going to be contradicted. In truth, it was hard to disagree with her, as not a single letter of hers had been found. Until I unearthed them, it was better for me to keep my opinions to myself. The only letters that existed, ironically, were the ones between Doris and me. It was imperative I do nothing to interfere with their free flow across the Irish Sea.

10

Ma was delighted she'd gone to Cork for the day. I was happy to report that I'd met Doris and that I'd safely put her on the boat at the North Wall terminal. It would be six months before she'd be back to visit Da's grave for his birthday in July. Even at this early stage I saw no reason why Ma shouldn't plan to be on her summer holidays when that time came around. It wasn't something she needed to worry about, one way or the other. I could tell she was happy that the obligation to Doris had been met and that it had been done without involving her.

I was in the good books with Ma.

— Good man, Pete—she said.—How are you fixed after the Christmas?

It was her way of inquiring was I all right for money.

— I'm fine, Ma—I said.—The only thing I need is a loan of the drill.

It was hanging up in the garage.

— That's your father's, you know—Ma said in a stern voice.—I want it back, now.

He was precious about his tools, but she was hardly expecting Da to come down from Glasnevin and make inquiries about who had borrowed it.

— I don't want you just walking off with his tools— she added.

I was upset that she thought I'd take it and not bring it back. He'd been dead two years and I hadn't borrowed as much as a screwdriver. I had all my own tools at home, but I didn't have a drill. I wasn't about to appropriate it because Da wasn't around to ask for it back. I was hurt at the insinuation.

— I won't take it—I said.—I'll borrow one someplace else.

— It's not like that, Pete, don't misunderstand me— she said.

She went on to explain that Gerard was now the man of the house. He had moved back home after Dympna and Michael, to be company for her. They had a love/hate relationship that was absolute. When things were going well between them, he called her "Anna," the only one of us to do that and get away with it. When things weren't going well, she was "Ma," and it sounded like a bee sting the way he said it. For her part, it was "Gerard" when she was on speaking terms with him and "the Gerry fella" when she wasn't. Since his return, she was doing her best to include him in all decision-making, and the disappearance of the drill, despite the fact that Gerard wouldn't even know how to turn it on, was the kind of rock their relationship could perish on.

I went out to the garage and saw that nothing had been disturbed since Da's death. All his old biscuit tins were in their place, each with its own unique inscription—assorted nails, rat traps and poisons, springs, car parts, hinges, bolts, and so on.

Hanging from the roof, like executed criminals, were some bigger pieces—a roll of barbed wire (we'd had it since I could walk and had never used it), a bicycle pump and tube, a lump hammer, a tenon saw, a sack full of pieces of gutter, and so on.

I reached for the Black & Decker and noticed that behind it was an old black briefcase. I recognized it as an attaché case from a production of *Juno and the Paycock* which we'd staged in 1968. In the drama, Da played Captain Boyle and I played his buddy, Joxer Daly. In the play, the captain inherits a fortune, and he procures a briefcase to keep all his papers and documents in. I pulled it out and I could tell it was full. It was bulging, but it was soft to the touch. It was held closed by means of twine wrapped around it and tied in a bow. I tugged at the string and released it. As I was about to open it, the thought struck me—it was the missing letters. He'd packed them into the case and stored them in the garage, where all his important things were kept. I brought it unopened into the living room and placed it on the table, under the light. I pulled back the flap to reveal a nest full to the brim. I spilled it out onto the table, but there wasn't a single letter of Doris's among the catch. It was memorabilia from our lives in the late 1960s, the years following on from Frankie's death, which became a resurrection for Da and, as a consequence, a new beginning for all of us.

Da had dreamed all his life of being Gary Cooper. In 1968, he lit the flame under that ambition and started a drama group, the St. Laurence O'Toole's Musical and Dramatic Society, also known as SLOT players. Ma was delighted with the new Da. She had been the one who'd kept the house ticking over as Da fell further and further into the black hole. The death of a child can destroy a marriage or can make it. In its wake, they found each other again. It may even be that it was the first time they were truly in love with one another. He certainly treated her better than he'd ever done before. In all this, he wanted Ma by his side, but she didn't have his energy. She had given too much of her passion in real life to expend what she had left on the stage.

Among the newspaper cuttings on the table were pictures of Belfast ablaze in August 1969. They were ones Ma had cut out from the *Irish Press* and the *Irish Independent*. Our house in Seville Place became a refugee center when the North exploded. We had the displaced Catholics of Belfast at our doorstep nightly. It was great for the adults, but there comes a point when you don't want to share your bedroom with strangers any more. It became commonplace to arrive home and find a note from Ma with instructions for me to share the pull-out bed in the front room with Shea or Johnny. Every arson attack in Belfast had profound implications for us in Dublin. Forty-four had always lacked privacy, and that seemed great when you were a kid. It wasn't so great when you were a teenager and there wasn't a corner of the house where you could bring a girlfriend.

So we did the adult thing and we left. Ita was the first to go, and she got married in August 1971. I followed her in October of the same year, and then Shea tied the knot in May 1972. The evacuation was completed by Johnny in 1974. In just over two years, the four eldest were all gone, happy in the knowledge that Ma and Da were on the crest of a second life together.

Ironically, among the papers scattered on the table before me were invitations to the various weddings, slightly yellowed with age and held together in a bundle by means of an elastic band. I slid one of the invitations from the pack and read it.

Mr. and Mrs. Frankie O'Donoghue invite you to the wedding of their daughter, Sheila, to Mr. Peter Sheridan at St. Anthony's Church, Clontarf, on Saturday, October 16, at 3 p.m., and afterwards to the Grand Hotel, Malahide. RSVP.

They were all there, preserved for posterity. I fished out another, and it surprised me.

*Miss Doris Johnson invites you to the wedding of her daughter,
Amanda, to Mr. Max Dryden, son of Albert and Elizabeth
Dryden, Park Street, Oldham. Nuptials will take place on Sat-
urday, June 10, at 3 p.m.*

I showed it to Ma. She couldn't read it without her glasses,
and so I read it out loud to her. When I'd finished, she said
nothing in response.

— Well, did you go?—I asked her.

— Yes, we both went—she said.—Why wouldn't we?

I turned the invitation over, and there on the back was a
message to Da.

*Dear Peter, I would love for you to give Amanda away if that's
acceptable. Let me know by return. Yours Doris.*

Why had Doris asked Peter to give her daughter away if he
wasn't the father? Once again the question loomed large in my
mind.

— So who gave Amanda away?—I asked.

Ma looked at me like I'd just revealed the third secret of Fa-
tima. She went scurrying for her glasses, and this time she
found them in the pocket of her cardigan.

— Let me see that—she said.

I handed it to her. She turned it over and read it to herself.
When she finished, she threw it on the table and shook her
head in disbelief. It seemed no matter what she did, Doris
would not go away.

Your father was livid that the wedding coincided with a big race meeting at the Curragh. It was the Irish Derby, I think. He fancied some horse in the race, and now he couldn't go. Do you know the fool I am, I thought it was Doris was getting married. He never said it was Amanda, he just said there was a wedding invitation from Doris and she wanted him to give her away. I don't know what got into me, but I thought it was Doris. I suppose I wanted it to be her. I'd love for her to have found someone to spend the rest of her life with. When Da said wedding, Amanda never entered my head. She was still a child to me. The picture in my head was Da walking down the aisle and handing Doris over to some man. It was a very odd image, but I was over the moon. I asked him the name of the man Doris was marrying, and he nearly spat his false teeth out.

— What do you mean?—says he.

— Who's her intended?—I said.

Well, I needn't tell you, there was a row after the mixup was sorted out. I couldn't believe he wanted to give Amanda away. I couldn't believe it after all we'd been through. I told him it wasn't his place, that it was up to her father to give her away. Then it struck me that maybe he was the father, and I asked him to tell me. He denied it, in fairness, but the damage was done. There hadn't been cross words between us in ages, but a wedding invitation from Doris and we were at it just like the good old days. I told him to go on his own, that I'd only spoil it for him. He said he'd only go if I went with him, and he had decided not to give Amanda away.

We went over to Blackburn, and down the aisle came Amanda on her mother's arm. It was my suggestion, and she thought it had come from Peter. You'd want to see her smiling over at him, you'd think he was Clark Gable. The vicar didn't want her doing it, but he wasn't to know that St. Peter had told her it was all right.

He was a lovely chap, her husband, what's this you call him, he had the high forehead that made him look intelligent. Max, that's it. Amanda and Max, they made a lovely couple, and her dress was out of this world. Da nearly died when the best man called on him to make a speech. He hadn't prepared anything, but he told one of his yarns and got them all laughing, and once he got them on his side they couldn't sit him down. Doesn't it take the Irish to get a wedding going? I never enjoyed a reception as much. I suppose, when it's not one of your own, you've nothing to worry about. I must have danced with every man in the place, including Uncle George. He was the first Black and Tan I ever danced with, that's for sure. I put him straight on the North, I can tell you, and he was going to join Sinn Féin by the time I was finished with him. Jesus, he could dance, and him seventy-five if he was a day. They're great ballroom dancers, the English, but they're a bit stiff at letting go. The singsong was a disaster until Da got up. He did his Bobby Darin thing, "Mack the Knife," and then what do you know but he called on me. I never sing but, Jesus, I couldn't let the side down. I was going to chance "A Nation Once Again," but I wasn't sure of the words. So I sang a Belfast one, "I'll Tell My Ma," it's a kids' song but it went down well. Then the manager of the hotel came in and told us we couldn't sing. Well, you know how prim Doris is, she lit on him. She read him the riot act. How dare he tell her not to sing! How dare he try and spoil her daughter's big day! How dare he embarrass her in front of visitors from overseas! Oh, there was smoke coming out of her ears, she was like a dragon. It took Da to calm her down and restore sanity.

We ended up back in Victoria Street, and the singsong went on half the night. At four o'clock in the morning, I got up to get a taxi, but Doris wouldn't hear of it. She insisted on us taking her bed, she didn't want us to leave. I wasn't too keen, but she said she could sleep in Amanda's room. I thought, What the hell, you only live once, so I rowed in with the idea. I knew it wasn't me she wanted in her bed, but I was too tired to care. Da and myself crawled up the stairs and got into the leaba. I never slept in a more comfortable bed in all my life. Isn't that strange, the last place on earth I wanted to sleep and it turns out to be the most comfortable? I slept the sleep of the dead that night.

The following morning was spent in a frantic search for Da's overcoat. It had gone missing overnight. He was sure he'd brought it from the hotel, but if he'd done that, where was it? We searched every room in the house, we searched them twice, there was no overcoat. I told him to try and remember the last time he had it. He remembered having it across his arm before we left the hotel. If that was the case, then it was lost somewhere between the hotel and Victoria Street. Da insisted on going back to the hotel. We were running late, but Da didn't care, he was like a demon. We got to the hotel, and Mr. Stuck-Up Nose from the night before was on duty. He took great pleasure in telling us that nothing had been handed in. I'd have gone to jail for this fella, only I didn't want to spend another night in England. So we made a dash for the train, and we caught it, and when we were on the boat, Da started to cry. I didn't know what was up. I thought he was upset at leaving your woman in Blackburn. It wasn't that at all, he was crying over a horse. He'd backed the horse in the Derby, the one he'd been waiting all year on, and I assumed it lost the race.

     —I backed the shagging winner—says he.—I had a tenner on it at seven-to-one.

     — Then you won seventy pounds—says I.—That's a lot of money.

     — The bloody docket—says he—it was in the right-hand pocket of the overcoat.

     He was like a child who'd burst his balloon. I gave him a hug and patted him on the head.

     Six days after we got back, the docket arrived in the post. Doris had sent it, of course. Some kindly neighbor had found the coat on the street and handed it in. I thought that was "my eye" for starters. She didn't want to send the coat, she said, because she didn't trust parcel post. So she was going to hold on to it until the next time Peter was in England. She thought he could collect it when he came to see United play. People were still talking about his speech at the wedding. It was all good arse-licking, and he couldn't see through it, God bless him. I told him it was her stole the coat.

     — Not at all—said he.—Why would she do that?

     — Because she's a bitch—says I—and I know how bitches behave.

     He wouldn't talk to me after that. I'd hurt his pride. He could be led up the garden path very easily, and he didn't know when he was being flattered.

It was obvious to me, but he couldn't see it. As long as it was just her letters, I hadn't too much to worry about, I suppose. It was the way she went on around him that drove me mad. He didn't have to do anything. He only had to sit there and she pumped up his ego. Just like he was the wheel of a bicycle. She'd pump until he nearly burst. She made a saint of him, and you know what they say about saints—they're very hard to live with.

It was two years before the coat was returned, and I played a part in it, unbeknownst to myself. By the mid-1970s, I was struggling as a young dramatist and theatre director. I worked at a series of jobs to support my young family and wrote in my spare time. Among these was a job at the greyhound track three nights a week, which Da had secured for me. It suited him down to the ground, because I collected him in my secondhand Mini car and drove over to Shelbourne Park. That meant he didn't have to take his car out of the garage. The thought that he was conserving fuel filled him with a delight usually reserved for children on Christmas morning. Petrol brought out the Shylock in Da. He valued it on equal terms with his blood.

One night on our way over to the track, he asked me for a cigarette. He was very antismoking and always on at Ma to give them up. He looked awful with a cigarette in his hand. I was a smoker, but I was filled with revulsion at the way he sucked the filter. He looked like a sly, devious old man. He didn't inhale properly and seemed to envelop himself in smoke. He started to cough and looked at me like he wanted to stop himself but couldn't.

— What are you smoking cigarettes for?—I asked him.

— I'm in trouble with the dames—he said.

He didn't elaborate before we reached Shelbourne Park. My job at the track was to collect the winning dockets from the various booths and bring them back to the control room for verification. Da was next to the general manager. He worked out the dividends for each race—the win, place, and forecast—and then he called them out over the loudspeaker system. It was strange listening to his calm, authoritative voice and knowing that he was in turmoil inside. I was walking under the new grandstand when I heard him announce the result of the sixth race.

— Here is the tote dividends on the sixth race. Dog six wins . . .

There was a pause and he went into the worst bout of coughing I've ever heard. He tried to get his voice back, but it only got worse. Finally, his colleague Ed Byrne came on and read out the dividends. It was the first time in twenty years at the dogs that he'd screwed up. After the races, we met in the car park.

— If I ever ask you for a cigarette again, you have my permission to cut out my tongue—he said in deadly earnest.

We got in the car and he asked me to take him to the North Wall. It was strange because he wasn't meeting anyone off the boat as far as I knew. When we got there, he asked me to pull in by the wall. He got out of the car and told me to go home. He'd walk to the Liverpool Bar to meet Ma. It seemed odd to leave him there, but who was I to argue.

— Who are you waiting for?—I asked him.

— I'm waiting for the boat to leave—he said.

I turned the car around and drove away. In my mirror, I saw him shield his eyes and look out to sea. A moving building glided across the top of the water past him—it was the Liverpool boat sailing out to sea. He took his cap off and started to wave it like he was saying goodbye to someone on board. I turned the ninety-degree bend onto Alexandra Road and he disappeared. I drove through East Wall and over Johnny Cullen's Hill into Seville Place.

I couldn't shake off the feeling that I'd abandoned him at the ferry terminal, so I turned the car around and went back. I was driving through the security gate at the bottom of Alexandra Road when I saw him walking towards me on the far side. Across his arm was an overcoat. I lowered my window and shouted over to him, but he was lost in his own thoughts. I did a U-turn and pulled up beside him. He got into the car and I could tell something had happened.

  — Who were you waving to on the boat?—I asked him.

  He pursed his lips and waited a moment.

  — Can I give you a piece of advice?—he said.

  — Of course you can—I answered.

  — Don't ever try and love two women—he said.— Don't try, because it's not possible.

  I knew the reference was to Doris, and I knew it was her he was waving to on the boat. Why would she come over to Ireland and not see him? I couldn't figure it out. I tried to prize more information from him, but he wasn't forthcoming. I even went into the Liverpool with him and had a drink, but Ma arrived soon afterwards, and that was an end to that. As I was leaving, he asked how Sheila and the kids were.

  — They're great—I said.

  — Be thankful for what you've got—he said, and winked at me.

  It was the only advice he ever gave me on how to stay happily married.

I wrote to Doris and asked her about the overcoat. She had indeed brought it to Dublin, but in order to keep her promise, she remained in the waiting area. That meant she was technically not in the country. She remained behind the barrier and waited for Peter. She waited for him to come and pick up his coat. If he did come she was hoping he would also come to England. She didn't mind if he brought Gerard and Paul with him to Blackburn. He couldn't let the family stand in his way for the rest of his life. Sooner or later, he would have to follow the dictates of his heart.

It was unfortunate that the dog-racing finished late and Peter missed the boat. She was certain he'd have left with her had he made it. He wrote saying how sorry he was to have missed her but he was glad to get his coat back. The night porter had given it to him. She was glad it was back in Dublin, but she was broken-hearted at her own banishment. She understood how much Frankie's death had changed things, but everyone had a right to personal happiness, and that included her and Peter. She asked him would they have to wait until Anna died before they could be together, and he said yes. The probability was fifty-fifty at best, and she didn't need to explain odds to Peter. For now, all she could do was wait until the big day came. She couldn't pray for it, that would be wrong. All she could do was wait.

The letters kept her from going insane. The radio, too, kept her informed and gave her things to write about. Whenever there was trouble, she would write and inquire if everyone was safe. It didn't matter how many times Peter told her that Dublin wasn't the scene of sectarian strife, she felt compelled to write. No amount of reassurance reassured her. It was as though the turbulence in Ireland was related to her in a personal way. For as long as "the troubles" persisted, she herself was a victim of them. She was at the wrong end of tribal hatred that made her union with Peter almost, but not entirely, impossible.

The Stardust tragedy provoked a rash of letters. It was Valentine's Eve, 1981, when she heard the news on Radio Éireann. A fire had broken out and destroyed a dance hall frequented by young people from all over Dublin's north side. Throughout the night and the following day, the death toll mounted. Teenagers who were present were being interviewed about what had happened. Some of them were from the Seville Place area. Doris was frantic that Gerard or Paul might have been caught up in it. Forty-eight young people lost their lives, but there were no Sheridans among the final list of the dead.

The years following brought huge changes to Seville Place. To everyone's surprise, Da took early retirement from CIE. For the workaholic he was, it confounded expectation. What would he do with his days now that he was free? Perhaps he would take up golf or go hill-climbing? Or become a professional punter and go racing every day? Maybe he'd take up acting professionally and join the Abbey Theatre? None of those things were on his list. Da reckoned there were enough jobs around the house to keep him going for the next ten years. First and foremost among these was the problem with the water pressure. Ma said she was putting on her hat and coat and emigrating if Da dug up any more water pipes.

On the first Monday of his retirement, he took on the water with gusto. He rescued a few old barrels from the back of the garage and painted them red and white, the colors of Dublin Corporation. He placed the barrels on the street and connected them with some weathered planks to keep the general public at bay. He sharpened the pickax and started to dig. He was on his own, a one-man roads department, battling great odds, a warrior standing alone in the mouth of the dragon, a diviner in search of water, the world's most precious commodity.

The search for the water pipes led to an unexpected family reunion. He dug for a week without success, but on the Saturday afternoon his luck changed. He backed a few winners and, buoyed by his success, he went out and dug with renewed vigor. He struck metal, and it rang out like an ancient church bell, the perfect ping of a Christian doing God's work, adding to the mystery of the world. That's how it was until the heavens opened. He stood there drenched to the skin and didn't know where the rain was coming from. It was gushing from the mains pipe, cascading forty feet into the air, as if he'd just struck oil. The water made a river of what had once been a street.

Emergency phone calls went out, and we all rushed to the scene of the disaster. When I arrived, Shea and Johnny were putting sandbags by the kitchen door to stem the flow. Gerard and Paul were inside with Ma, filling buckets and basins and throwing them down the sink. A crowd had gathered at the corner of Emerald Street and Seville Place, to watch. Da, meanwhile, had taken refuge in the garage to ponder his next move. If he called the Corporation, he could be arrested and put in jail for digging up the street.

The problem was that, when he'd struck the pipe, he'd dislodged a stop nut. Without it, there was no chance of plugging the leak. I rounded up all the available grandchildren—Rossa and Fiachra, Naomi and Kirsten (Shea's two daughters), and Carol (Johnny's eldest). I got five plastic sacks and made raincoats from them. I described what they were to look for and sent them out into the jaws of the torrent. There was a five-pound reward on offer if they found it. Less than two minutes later, Rossa was in the back door with the nut in his hand, but he wouldn't give it to his granddad until I paid over the money.

Returning the nut to its slot was impossible. The pressure of the water was too intense. Da came up with a solution. He got Shea, Johnny, and me to lean on him and push down as he put his hand into the hole. We were drenched to the skin, all four of us, but Da was sure it was going to work. It's amazing what the threat of jail will bring out in a man. Da had no feeling left in his hand, it was numb from the effects of the water. We convinced him to give Shea a go with the nut. At the second attempt, Shea managed to plug the pipe and stem the cascade. We wasted no time in filling in the hole, removing the barrels, and clearing the site of any evidence that would connect Da to the mess.

That afternoon, Ma took charge of his retirement. She went uptown and came home with a brochure, which she threw on the table in front of him.

— We're going to visit Dympna and Michael, and I don't want any arguments about it—Ma said.

Da was taken aback, but he stayed outwardly calm.

— Dympna and Michael in Melbourne—he said.

— That's right, Da, Melbourne, Arsetralia, to be precise—she said.

— What about the lodgers?—Da inquired.

Ma still had four under her roof whom she catered for. Mrs McErlean and her wee daughter, Anne, refugees from Belfast were still with us. She also had Noel O'Donnell, a barman from Wexford (he brought Da home a crate of Harp lager every Saturday night), and a builder from Cavan, Ciaran O'Reilly (who wanted to be an actor like Da).

— I'm letting the lodgers go—she said.

It took him completely by surprise.

— You're letting them go for good?—he asked in a disbelieving way.

— Yes—Ma said—if you can retire, so can I.

There was great excitement when they got back from Down Under. They couldn't stop talking about Australia. Everything about it appealed to them. The cost of living, the weather, the price of beer, the people, the beaches, the restaurants, Sydney

Harbor, Melbourne Cricket Ground, the Aussie accent, the huge Irish community, and especially meeting Dympna and Michael, who threw parties in their honor and made them feel like very special guests, and somehow it made them feel very special to each other in a way they hadn't felt before.

Ma showed off pictures of Da swimming on Manley Beach. Da pointed to little flecks in the background and said they were white sharks. Rossa and Fiachra were very impressed and thought he was the bravest granddad in the world. He encouraged their adulation, greatly.

— What was the sea like, Granddad?—they asked him.

I thought he was going to say soup.

— It was dangerous—he said—very dangerous and very scary.

The boys were impressed enough that they went running out to tell all their friends on the street.

Da showed pictures of Ma standing outside Sydney Opera House.

— What was it like, Ma?—I asked her.

— Out of this world, Peter, simply out of this world—she said.

There were photographs of Da with his hand over Ma's shoulder and her hand around his waist. They were photographs of lovers. Their skins were touching. The sun had burnt away all past sadness. They were in each other's grip, holding on to each other, not wanting to let go. They were sixteen, at a fun fair, and he'd just won a teddy bear at the shooting gallery. Everyone wanted to take their photograph, and they were happy to pose for every click. Ma had planned it as a retirement party and it turned out to be her honeymoon. Da had gone out of a sense of duty and now he wanted to emigrate there.

— A country for old people who want to stay young—he called it.

— We don't know how to live here—Ma said—just don't know how to live.

So Ma let the lodgers go, as she'd promised, and within a month she'd taken a part-time job in the bar of the North Star Hotel. She valued having her independent few shillings as she valued her life. Da valued it, too, of course. On his way back from the dog track (I had long since left it, in the full-time pursuit of a career in the theatre), Ma had his pint ready and waiting on the counter, and he didn't have to put his hand in his pocket to pay for it. If he could have found her a part-time job in a bookie's during the day, his world would have been complete.

Life as a bar lady was a holiday for Ma after the stresses and strains of running a boarding house. Not that the North Star Hotel didn't get its fair share of head cases from Sheriff Street and the docks. Ma served them, and they never tried to rob the hotel when she was on duty out of respect for Da's service to the community—he'd taught many of the city's leading criminals how to swim and play basketball.

That was how it stood until the night of the attack. It was a Wednesday evening, coming up to half past ten, the bar was slack, and she decided it was time to pull Da's pint. She held the glass in her left hand, put it under the Guinness tap, and raised her right hand to pull the drink. Just then, she felt like someone had come in behind the counter and grabbed her by the arm. She was so paralyzed she couldn't turn to see who it was. She tried to call the manager, Mr. McKay, but her voice wouldn't work.

A local came into the bar and ordered a drink. He knew by her reaction that there was something wrong. He came in behind the counter and put her sitting on a stool. He called the manager, and they fed her some whiskey. By the time Da arrived, ten minutes later, the drama was over. She wanted to work on, of course, but Da brought her home. The next day, she had no feeling down her right-hand side, and her speech was slightly slurred. She went to the hospital for tests and they kept her in. She'd had a mild stroke, a warning shot across her bow telling her it was time to start taking things easy.

Ma was home from the hospital about a week when Da had a similar attack down his left-hand side. He was over at the dog track, calculating the dividends, when he felt like he'd been hit by a truck. He knew what it was because of Ma, and he had the sense to get the duty manager to drive him to the hospital. He'd had a stroke in sympathy with Ma. When he got home, it was like they were two halves of one person. What was good for Ma was bad for him, and vice versa. He couldn't hold his fork, and Ma couldn't hold her knife. If they hadn't been getting on so well, they would have divorced. Had it not been for their Australian honeymoon, their strokes might have killed them. On the other hand, Australia might have brought it all on. Maybe they'd had a glimpse of a stress-free life in the sun, and now they were back in the gray reality of Ireland having to face weather that was a permanent reminder of death.

Ma's health went from bad to worse. Looking after the drafty old house in Seville Place didn't help. She'd always had a bad chest from the cigarettes, and the four flights of stairs were a killer. So they sold up and moved out of the parish. It was an emotional farewell for them and for all of us. It was time to go, and we all turned up and helped with the move to Carleton Road, a mile farther north, in the suburb of Marino. After the stroke, Da hung up his car keys, but luckily their new house was on the bus route to all the important bingo halls on the north side.

Shortly after they moved, I brought Ma to the Blackrock Clinic. The specialist, who had eight letters after his name and charged accordingly, told her she'd die if she didn't quit smoking. She was suffering from emphysema, and there was damage to her windpipes that couldn't be repaired. She could halt the deterioration if she quit the cigarettes, but the picture was very grim if she didn't. He gave her a machine called a nebulizer to help her with her breathing. She was to use it four times a day, and it came in its own little case so she could take it with her wherever she went.

Ma hated the nebulizer and refused to use it. To deflect attention from it, she made a ceremony of throwing her cigarettes in the bin, vowing never to smoke another one as long as she lived. Da wasn't having any of it. He put the nebulizer on the table and put the mask over her face. She found it gave her back some breath. She used it for a few days and found that she was running up the stairs again. Her morning cough improved so much she didn't need to hold on to the table any more. The chief cause of the improvement was undoubtedly the nebulizer, and Ma became a great champion of it. The nebulizer replaced the cigarettes as Ma's "one and only vice."

— That machine is the only bit of comfort I have.

Despite all the worry over her health, Ma was very public about her ailments. As well as the stroke and the emphysema, there were a series of things she complained about in rotation. On her feet were the corns and the fallen arches, and she attended the chiropodist, Mr. Mullen, for those. She had a crooked pelvis and attended the chiropractor, Alan, whom she insisted on calling a psychopractor. She stopped going to him only after he mistakenly cracked one of her ribs during a manipulation. She had a lower-back problem that Miss Kennedy, the physiotherapist (a lovely girl, just out of college), treated for her. Then she had her local GP, Murnane, who looked after colds, flus, migraines, earache, etc. She had a tablet for every condition, and she knew them all by color only. If it was her bronchitis, it had to be the red-and-black capsules; and if it was a migraine, then the yellow ones with the blue writing were the solution. Ma never made a secret of her health problems, and because she talked about them so much, she forgot from one day to the next what her ailments were.

Da, on the other hand, was as secretive as you could get. He was embarrassed that people knew of his stroke. For a man who spent so much of his life in promoting community activity, he hated when the spotlight fell on him. He loved being at the center of the party, and he had no problem hogging the limelight on a stage. He just hated being the object of anyone's sympathy. He couldn't cope with sickness, and when he was unwell he tried to isolate himself as best he could.

He didn't trust the specialists and always put his own interpretation on what they told him. When advised that gentle walking would be good for his heart, he interpreted this as meaning a spin on the bike would be even better. If walking was good, cycling was twice as good! Da knew all about blood pressure, having backed his fair share of losers in his time, so he monitored his own progress in the wake of the stroke. He didn't need to pay a specialist to tell him things he knew already. He did what was right for him. He kept fit, stayed away from cigarettes, cut down on the pints of Guinness, and watched for fat in his food. The main plank in his health strategy was to avoid doctors at all costs.

He must have been feeling pretty awful in the days leading up to his death. He hadn't looked well for months, that was true. There didn't seem to be any obvious stress in his life. He didn't owe any money, the bills were paid, and he and Ma were getting on better than ever. Unless there was pressure from Doris that we didn't know about. She may not have been able to cope with her continued banishment. Maybe he had told her he was sick and she sensed he would die before her. It may have been that something in her letters hastened his demise.

I gathered up the papers I'd spilled out onto the table and started to return them to the attaché case. It was astonishing how much of the past Da had preserved. I stuffed the wedding invitations, the newspaper cuttings and the old theatre programs into the front pouch. They wouldn't fit. No matter how I tried I couldn't get them to go back in as they'd come out. I called on Ma for help and, between the two of us, we failed miserably.

— There was no one like your father for packing a case—she said.

In the end, we had to transfer some of the documents to one of his shoe boxes in the press. If we ever needed something to show how much we missed him, this was it. I asked Ma how he'd been in the days preceding his collapse.

We had decided on another trip to Arsetralia. I thought it might buck him up. He suggested we stop over in Bangkok for a few days. I thought we might need injections for malaria, so I fixed an appointment with the doctor. He gave us a clean bill of health. I was worried about the electricity in Bangkok, on account of the nebulizer. I wanted to make sure I could plug it in. I rang the embassy of Thailand. It was Da got the number for me, out of the phone book. I tried to explain to the girl, but she didn't understand me. So I spelled out "nebulizer" for her. She still didn't understand what I was talking about. I tried to pass the phone to Da, but he was doubled-up, laughing.

— *What's so bloody funny?—I asked him.*

He couldn't talk, of course, and I got annoyed with him. I told the girl to hold on because my husband was acting like a child.

— Maybe she thinks it's a sex toy—he said.

— You have sex on the brain—I said—and it's worse you're getting with age.

I just wanted to know a simple answer to a simple question, and he was turning it into an orgy. I slammed down the phone in disgust. That brought him to his senses. He rang the girl back and got the information. I was sorry then I'd given out to him because he did look awful. I would have suggested going back to the specialist, only we'd been to the doctor and his blood pressure was all right. I'm sorry now I didn't follow my instincts. If I had, he might still be alive. It's terrible to think the pneumonia was inside attacking him and none of us knew. If only he'd said something. Two words, that would have done, I'm sick, that's all it would have taken. Instead of that, I'm down at the shops buying lamb chops and turnip for the dinner and he's on his way to meet God. I hate to think of him lying on the floor with the life pouring out of him. I've often wondered what his last thoughts were. I wonder was he thinking about Arsetralia. Maybe he was thinking about the racing result he'd marked. No Submission, it sums him up in a way. He was always a fighter. He boxed for Ireland as a schoolboy, but you know that. He fought for all of us. I hope he had nice thoughts at the end. I hope he wasn't struggling. I can't stand to think of him lying on the floor wondering where the hell I was. I don't think he was. I think he was at peace. I think he was dead before he hit the floor. I hope he was. That's my hope, that he didn't suffer at the end. He deserved that.

11

Doris took the plunge and became a Catholic. She was afraid there might be two parts to heaven, a Catholic one and a Protestant one. It was hard to imagine that heaven would be split in two like Belfast, with a peace line running down the middle separating the factions. If it was, she was going fully prepared. She had put so much faith in being with Peter after Anna died, and it had backfired on her. She wasn't going to make the same mistake with regard to the afterlife. Doris had no intention of spending eternity separated from Peter by a concrete wall.

She embraced her new religion with the zeal of a convert. At her request, I brought her to mass on the occasion of her July visit to celebrate Peter's birthday. I chose the church of St. Laurence O'Toole's for obvious reasons. We knelt in a pew that bore the inscription "Matt Talbot prayed here." Once the bell sounded for the start of mass, Doris focused on the altar and threw herself into the responses. She enunciated at a level just short of too loud, and in so doing she reminded me of Billy the Hogger, a neighbor from the old days who used to shout out the Latin hymns at the top of his voice. In between the responses, she prayed with an intensity that defied interruption. The congregation was small, no more than twenty people. This was the altar where I'd served mass and learnt my first foreign words:

Ad deum qui laetificat
Juventutem meum

You had to be ten minutes early for Sunday mass when I was an altar boy or you wouldn't get a seat. So much of our family history was played out here, the sad occasions and the happy ones. I'd made my First Holy Communion here, and my Confirmation, too. This was where we brought Frankie's coffin on a day when the whole of Dublin seemed to be sandwiched between its walls. It was down this aisle that Ita walked with Da in August 1971, when she became the first of us to get married. She carried a bunch of white gardenia, and I could recall their sweet smell if I closed my eyes.

It was ironic to be kneeling here with Doris when the church's popularity was so clearly on the wane. She was trying to embrace the mystery of it when the mystery had disappeared. The church had done nothing to save the docks, and now the community it had abandoned was abandoning it. There was no one left to preach to. The stragglers were taking out insurance on the next life, that was all. Doris was there out of fear that she might lose Peter again. Her faith recalled the old days. If she didn't believe, she'd be punished for all eternity. It was a simple faith, and it was all the more powerful for that simplicity. It flowed from the certainty of her own resurrection. It was just like the mass, the bread representing the food of life, and the host the miracle of its transformation into the body of Christ.

Doris believed that she would one day share heaven with Peter. Matt Talbot had knelt here with chains strapped to his body but they were no more real than the emotional ones that enveloped Doris. Someday God would relieve her of them and bring her true happiness. She would spend eternity with the man she loved as the reward for her earthly banishment.

I have no idea where she saw Anna in all this, if she saw her at all. I prayed that God would find a solution to the conundrum, because I couldn't see it. I prayed for Da, too, and though I missed him, I hoped it would be a while before I saw him again. When I thought of him, it was a distant sensation. His soul was gone, and the nearest I got to it was looking into Doris's face. Kneeling with my head bowed at the consecration bells, I remembered him as man who never wore his religion on his sleeve. To him religion was not a public thing, it was the private measure of a person. "Don't ever be too proud to get down on your knees and pray" was the advice he'd offered when I told him I'd stopped going to mass. He didn't try to get me to reverse my decision, he offered simple words that I could recall thirty years on. I was happy to kneel in St. Laurence O'Toole's Church and remember him on the occasion of his seventy-fourth birthday. I was happy to receive the Eucharist in remembrance of all the meals he fought so hard to put on our table. At the conclusion of mass, I was happy to accept the priest's blessing as a blessing from him.

We left the church and walked down Sheriff Street. Most of the flats had been evacuated and were waiting to be demolished. It looked like a ghost town from a cowboy film. It was hard to believe Doris had once chased me along this street, to the cheers of my school pals. It now stood waiting for its final execution.

— Do people still sing in the pubs, or has all that changed?—Doris asked me.

There's no singing on death row, only silence.

— Yes, they do—I said—but not down here.

We walked on past the site of the Oriel Hall, where we'd staged the plays of Sean O'Casey. It was almost a row of red-bricked houses, a sign of future regeneration, I hoped. We walked from there on up past the railway station where she'd met Peter and shared corned-beef sandwiches with him. She had become a Catholic, but she was less a part of this city than when she was a naïve Protestant girl of twenty-four. She was divorced from what was taking shape beneath the cranes that dotted the skyline. I brought her to Bewley's of Westmoreland Street, and she basked in the decor, which brought her back to something of the old city she recognized.

— How is Anna's health?—she asked.

I was glad she'd inquired, and glad to report that Ma was fighting fit.

— Your father's letters were always full of her ailments—she added.

It was true, of course. Ma always had a sickness on the go. She was a hypochondriac, to be honest, and though I could admit that to myself, I didn't want Doris using it as a stick to poke fun at her.

— She had a stroke—I said with gravitas—but she never complained about it.

Doris looked contrite and didn't respond. She studied her sticky bun before she took a knife to it and plunged it in. Did she imagine it was Anna's heart? She stuffed her mouth with the cake and slurped her tea to wash it down.

— I were very jealous of Anna's stroke—she said.

Peter told me all about it. You know what he were like with a good story, he squeezed every last drop out of it. I could see it happening the way he wrote it. It brought them closer together. I felt left out, to be honest. It would have been nice to have one. A stroke is such a personal thing. I don't mind admitting I was jealous.

After his attack, he told me he could only get drunk down one side of his body. I thought that were awful. In my mind I could picture one half of him out of control, like he were taking a fit, and the other side calm. I was afraid the drunk side would win the war. I pleaded with him to cut down on what he drank. I needn't tell you what he said in reply. What sort of a fool am I, that I swallowed his blarney? Can you believe I fell for it? I never had much of a sense of humor, it had been beaten out of me, you see. Not physically, mind, but every other way. My father drained it from me, and Peter gave it back to me. I couldn't tell he was joking, because I couldn't see him. Sometimes you have to see a person's face, you have to look into their eyes to know if they're serious. I could always tell with Peter when I had him there in front of me. I could have lied about having a stroke, could have made it up, of course, but I'm no good at lying. I got so depressed that I wrote and broke it off. Posted it at the bottom of Victoria Street and went home and had a good cry. Then I got so upset I decided to write to Peter and tell him what I'd done. He was the only person I could talk to. The pad came out and I started to write and I asked him what was I going to do now that I'd stopped writing to him. I knew I were mad. I ran down to the post box and waited for the van. When it came, I asked the driver to return my letter, but he said he couldn't do that, because it were against the law. Once I'd put it through the slot, it became the property of the Royal Mail. Technically, it belonged to the Queen, so I pleaded with him, as one of her loyal subjects, to give me back my letter or I'd lie down on the ground in front of the van and let him drive over me. That persuaded him, and he found it for me.

I went home and threw it in the fire. It were a lucky escape, and I never mentioned it to Peter. I didn't want to upset him. He got enough of a fright with the stroke. He had it in sympathy with Anna, because that's what couples do. They become so close they share one another's illnesses. Sometimes I regret that I didn't put more pressure on him to leave. He might still be alive if I'd done that. That would have been better for all of us, if he were still alive.

He was too busy looking after Anna's ailments to think about his own. I've never been a day sick in my life. My mother survived into her ninety-second year. It runs in our family. I could have looked after Peter. They were thinking of settling in Australia. The weather appealed to Peter, and they have horse racing, too. I think it was the best holiday they ever had. Then they even had their strokes together. I couldn't compete with that. I could talk about what was on the radio. The shipping forecast was read out every night, and I loved to imagine my bed were on the Irish Sea, and I loved the drama of a good wind, blowing me from Wexford up to Dundalk and back down to Dublin. Hecto pascals and gusting winds and gale-force warnings, such lovely drama. The shipping forecast is still my favorite, I know bits of it by heart. Malin Head to Loop Head to Carnsore Point. Such lovely names. It were as good as a play sometimes. In fact, it were better than a lot of the plays they had on. I never wrote to Peter about the shipping forecast, because it were just my imagination. I'm sorry now I didn't. I'm sorry my bed wasn't a boat that brought me to Dublin, because I could have nursed him. I did a course in first aid, just before the war. I'd been trained to save people, and I could have saved Peter. It's tragic I never got the chance. I should have taken it. It were silly to lie in my bed thinking about it when I could have done it. It's the biggest regret of my life. I should have ignored my banishment and come to him.

Dublin had become a pilgrimage. Everything was carried out like it had been ordained in heaven. The ritual began the day before sailing, when Doris chose her roses at a flower shop in Blackburn. She picked a red as close to the jersey of Manchester United as it was possible to get. Five minutes before leaving the house, she filled her flask with tea and wrapped the corned-beef sandwiches in foil. On her arrival in Dublin, she followed the route laid down by Peter the day the car wouldn't start. Along the East Wall Road and up through Ballybough became the pilgrim path. The church had once bestowed indulgences for such effort. Doris didn't care. For her it was a day of remembrance, she wasn't looking for a reward. That would come in the next life. She had to wait until she was called, however far away that might be. She had promised Peter never to take her own life. The odds were she could live a long time.

I thought of Matt Talbot. He'd been found in Granby Row, off Parnell Square, wrapped in chains. He'd pushed himself to the limits of endurance. Around the streets of Dublin he'd stomped from church to church, cramming in as many masses as he could. In the end, he'd paid for it with his life. Doris was following in his footsteps. Her pilgrimage was a marathon for a woman in her seventies. To perish on the streets of Dublin would be the perfect ending to her story. She had become the great Catholic mother of the book she treasured so much. She could become the great Catholic wife, too, if God would take her to Peter. She had to get there before Anna. All she could do was push herself to the limit and hope for the best.

It was all building nicely to a row in the next life. I felt sorry for Doris, but I hoped Ma got there before her. Anything else seemed like a recipe for disaster. It would be a repeat of the awful scene in Madigan's Pub with the roles reversed. Ma had prayed always for peace, it was her great wish. We had laid Da in his grave with the salutation that he "rest in peace." As things were developing on earth, it seemed likely that would prove to be a temporary condition only.

— Have you put me into your book?—Doris asked.

I'd just finished writing a memoir of growing up in Seville Place in the 1960s. I wasn't aware I'd told her about it. I didn't even have a title for the book. Perhaps I'd mentioned it in one of my letters. On reflection, however, I knew I hadn't. I was intrigued she knew anything about it.

— How did you know about my book?—I asked her.

— You mentioned it on the radio—she said.—I think it was the Arts Show with Mike Murphy.

I was on talking about the play I'd directed and I only mentioned the book in passing. Nothing concerned with our family escaped her attention. She had been receiving information on us from Peter's letters for over forty years, and since his death, I had breached that gap. Her question about the book was bold and inquisitive. Indeed, I had agonized over whether to include her story or not. In the end, I felt it deserved a book by itself. I could hardly tell it in a time frame as restrictive as the 1960s, the period of my childhood memoir. The story of Doris and our family would have to wait for another day.

— I left you out because I'm going to write something about you and Peter—I said.

— That could be a long book—she said—that could be an epic.

— I'll probably base it around the letters—I said.

I was sure I'd said something wrong. She looked hurt and sad. She looked at me with doleful eyes like I'd scolded her.

— That will be a hard book to write—she said.

I had no doubt about its difficulty. It was an adult story, and I wouldn't be able to hide behind the child in telling it. That would be the challenge of it. I looked forward to taking it on.

— There are no letters—Doris said.—Your father and I destroyed them.

— Why did he destroy the letters?—I asked.

— He didn't want you getting your hands on them—she said.

It was hard to believe. He was a keeper of things. He put things in biscuit tins and envelopes and shoe boxes. He preserved the past, he protected the record. The fact that he'd put them to the sword indicated a clear motive of some kind, but I couldn't, for the life of me, figure out what it was.

He wrote and told me to burn them. He was preparing to leave Anna, I know that now, but I didn't know it at the time. How did I not see it? He wrote and told me to make a pile of all his letters. I was to set them ablaze, just like a funeral pyre. I was to do it in Blackburn, and he would do it in Dublin. He suggested the Wednesday at twelve o'clock. I set fire to them out the back, and when they were all burnt I dug a hole and buried the cinders. I'm sure they're still there, but I haven't checked. Why would he destroy the past if it wasn't to make a new future? I'm sorry now I burnt them, because I've nothing of him left. If I had the letters, I could take them out and read them. I used to envy Catholics that they married for life. Not any more, because I'm a Catholic, too. He wrote to me with a proposal the summer we met in Amiens Street. I had that letter for a long time. I burnt it with all the others. I have the one from Anna giving me the bad news. I don't like to read it, for obvious reasons. It makes me angry more than sad. I'd like to have been at the funeral. Peter would have wanted me there, he told me that once. He didn't tell me to come, but I should have known. That's my biggest regret. That I didn't come. He'd still be alive if I'd done that. Now it's back to waiting again. It won't be that much longer, God willing. With any luck I'll have a stroke, but I don't pray for one. If it comes, it comes, and if it doesn't, it doesn't. I'll be back here in January if God spares me. I must check the winter sailing times as soon as they come out. I like to plan in advance. I'll write and let you know when I'm coming. You write and tell me all about your book. I won't burn your letters, I promise. Not even if you tell me. I'll never make a funeral pyre of letters from Dublin again, you can be sure of that.

It was hard to believe their correspondence was gone. Not a single letter remained. Nobody had stood with her and forced her to strike the match, and she had preserved nothing. I felt saddened that I would never get to read them. The mystery of their disappearance had been explained, but the mystery of their content deepened. My curiosity had been dealt a terrible blow. The only way I could satisfy it now was through an act of the imagination.

I brought the manuscript of my book up to Ma's. I didn't really care what anyone else in the world thought of it. If Ma gave it the stamp of approval, that was all that mattered to me. I presented her with the book and gave her the news about the letters. She broke out all over in girlish delight.

— Good on you, Da, you did something right—she yelped and punched the air.

I hadn't seen her so animated since Dundalk won the FAI cup in 1988. She swooped in from the kitchen with the teapot poised. She started to pour from two feet in the air and brought the spout down as the cup began to fill. She completed the task without spilling a drop.

— What used you say, Da, the cup that cheers but doesn't inebriate—Ma said.

She was drunk with the news. She was like a bird who'd had a weight strapped to her claw and had forgotten she could fly. She was released into the air and had found freedom again. She was enjoying its sweet taste to the full.

— I can die happy now—she said.

The letters had been hanging over her head like a wrecking ball, and now they were no more. He destroyed something precious, and in so doing he had committed himself to her, not just for what was left of this life, but for all eternity. When it really mattered, he'd made amends for his infidelity. The destruction of the letters was his message of love from beyond the grave.

Ma recounted an incident that took place not long before his death. She remembered it was a Wednesday, because she'd gone to the post office to do the Lotto, which was worth over two million. When she came home, he was out in the back garden burning rubbish. She thought it odd, because he usually managed to fill the house with smoke when he lit a fire in the garden. The house was clear but the garden was covered in smuts. He was sitting on a chair poking the embers with a stick. The garden looked like it was full of black snow. She asked him what he was doing, and he said he was burning some old papers. She realized now the black snowflakes were Doris's letters. They floated up into the sky and out of her life.

— Why didn't he tell you what he was doing?—I asked.

— Why do you think? she asked straight back.

I shrugged my shoulders. In truth, I couldn't imagine why he would conceal it from her.

— He knew he was dying and was afraid to tell me—she said.

It made terrifying sense. Even at the end, he was afraid of love. He was much more at home with anger, rage, hatred, and obsession. Even at the eleventh hour, he had to make his amends in secret in case he gave the game away.

— Do you really think he knew?—I asked.

— Yes, I do—she said—I'm sure now that he knew.

He was such a gregarious man, and yet he must have been so lonely in those last days. He put his house in order and prepared himself for an exit. He squared up to meet his Maker, and then he left in a great hurry. I looked at the carpet where he'd fallen. I looked over at Ma, who was sitting at the table with her reading glasses on. She was leaning over the manuscript, and I was so nervous I got up to leave.

— Is the quare one in this?—Ma asked.

I explained that I'd left Doris out but would return to her story at another time.

— Well, you needn't publish that until after I'm gone—she said.

I knew she was serious when she looked over the rim of her glasses at me.

— That could be a long time away—I said.

She tapped her chest with her finger and gave a little cough to remind me of her mortality.

— I'll be dead before you know it, Pete—she said.

I tried to imagine the world without Ma. What would happen to bingo as we know it? How would the numbers have the courage to come out of the drum if they knew Ma wasn't in the hall? She had personal relationships with so many of them—nineteen, forty-four, fifty-one, and seventy. She loved and hated them in equal measure, but you can be sure they knew she was there. She would have to negotiate her withdrawal from life. She would grow old slowly, receive the check from the President on her hundredth birthday, we would burn up the years alongside her, and by the time she passed away we, too, would be old. It was enough to lose one parent, and I never wanted to think of the world without Ma. Amen.

— You got this wrong—she said with her finger on the page.—I never went into the Ball Alley Pub and bought your father a half-dozen Guinness.

I would have taken my oath on a stack of Bibles she'd gone to the Ball Alley for him. It was a bad omen for the rest of the book.

— If I wanted to get him Guinness, I'd have gone to the off-license, where it was half the price.

The look of disbelief on her face was priceless. I tried my best to suppress a laugh, but in the end it came bursting forth like an unstoppable fart. It took me some time to regain my composure. When I did, Ma was still looking at me with a very cross expression on her face.

— Answer me this—she said—do you want to get the book right or do you want to get it wrong?

Ma gave the book her seal of approval.

— I'm going to pass this—she said when she'd finished reading it.

Then she went through the list of whys. Why did I have to put in it that we kept a potty under the bed? Why did I have to describe Da's toilet in such awful detail? Why did I have to show him cutting up the phone directory for toilet paper? Why did I have to say they met every night in the Liverpool Bar for a drink? Could I not even vary where they went? Despite the whys, she was passing it, and I could breathe again.

At her suggestion, I called the book 44. When the cover design arrived, with me as a child at the front door of Seville Place, I rushed down to show it to her. The window cleaner was at work, so the front door was open. As soon as I stepped into the hall, I sensed something strange. I made my way to the sitting room, and Ma was in an armchair watching *Countdown* on the television. From behind her back, smoke was drifting up towards the ceiling.

— You're smoking, Ma—I said in complete disbelief.

— No, I'm not—she replied.

Across from her on the couch was an ashtray with three or four butts in it. Before I had time to allude to the damning evidence she came straight in.

— They must be Gerry's—she said.

I knew Gerard smoked, but I would have bet against him wearing pink lipstick. I sat down and watched the smoke pouring out from behind her. She continued to pretend it wasn't there. I realized her dignity was at stake, so I left the room and went out to the garden. I pottered around for about five minutes before I came back in. Ma was sitting at the table connected to the nebulizer.

— When did you go back on the cigarettes?—I asked.

— I never gave them up—she said.

I sat down to deliver the lecture, but I could only smile. I'd never given out to her in my life, and I wasn't going to start now. As long as she continued with her nebulizer, I figured, she couldn't go far wrong. She'd always had a great weakness for the cigarettes—the drinking and the gambling were purely periodic—and wasn't she entitled to at least one permanent vice in her life.

— What would Da say if he was here now?—I said. It was about as cross as I could get.

— What do you think he'd say?—I repeated.

She switched off the nebulizer and let the whirr of it die away.

— I think he'd say he misses me, that's what I think he'd say.

Ma turned the book launch into a great family occasion. They came from Dublin and Dundalk, Ardee, Knockbridge and Belfast. Johnny's band played after the speeches, and everyone danced. It was just like a proper wedding. With an eye for publicity, Ma posed for the camera. She insisted on reading the book in every photograph. When one of the press men pointed out that the book was, in fact, upside down, she went into paroxysms of laughter. That was the photo that made the front pages and all the social columns, too.

I was due to leave on a tour to promote the book. Ma asked me if I could postpone it until after her birthday. Delighted as I was to comply, it was the strangest thing, because Ma never made a fuss of her birthday. I knew her reluctance to celebrate it was tied up in the circumstances of her birth. We never knew our maternal grandmother, naturally, so it never impinged when we were small children. All we knew was that you got to blow out candles on your birthday and we couldn't understand Ma's lack of enthusiasm for her big day. Not even the landmark birthdays of sixty and seventy were marked in a special way. As I got older, I came to understand and accept it.

We gathered in Carleton Road on the 8th of May, 1999, children and grandchildren, to celebrate Ma's seventy-eighth birthday. Ita had traveled up from Cork, Shea had flown in from London, Johnny had canceled a gig for the band, and I'd put off my trip to the West Coast of America. Indeed, Ma herself had put back a hospital appointment to be free on the day. She was due in for tests, because the pain in her lower back had not responded to physiotherapy. She put on her best blue suit, and Ita spent time on her makeup, but despite all the effort, Ma couldn't hide her upset. She'd had a bad dream about Da and couldn't shake it off. He'd come into the North Star Hotel and there was no pint ready for him. She rushed up the bar to serve him, but he didn't recognize her. She tried to get his attention, but he turned away and ignored her. She couldn't hide her distress in recounting it. She was as upset as if she'd found him dead on the floor.

I set off for San Francisco on the Sunday, and Ma went in for her tests on the Monday. It was good to spend time in the adopted city of my elder son, Rossa. He showed me around and became my guide. He had a wide circle of friends whom I had never met, and they came from every corner of the globe. Many of them attended a reading I gave in a bookstore with the wonderful name of A Clean Well-Lighted Place. As so often on these occasions, I didn't actually read but told stories. I usually started with one of Da's mad escapades—fixing the water pressure or erecting the television aerial—but on this occasion I started with Ma and stayed with her all night. In the course of one anecdote, I referred to her as a warrior, and it was the first time I'd found a word that described her.

Later that evening, Rossa surprised me.

— I'm coming home to see Granny—he said.

— Wait until Christmas, when you were coming home anyway—I advised him.

— I don't want to wait, I'm coming home now—he said.

Ma had brought us together on her birthday to say goodbye. That was the meaning of her dream. She was missing Da and wanted to be with him. She didn't want to leave us, of course, and under cover of her birthday, that's what she was telling us. In our hearts we all knew, but it was unexpressed. There are some things not even words can hide, however, and despite my own attempts to protect Rossa from the truth, he, too, knew in his heart.

The following day, when I was due to fly to Los Angeles, I got a phone call from Paul. The tests had not gone well. Her condition was terminal. At best, she had ten days to live. I canceled the tour and flew straight back to Dublin. Sixteen hours later, I walked with Rossa and Sheila into Ma's room at the Blackrock Clinic.

— Good God, Rossa, what are you doing here?— she said.

He wasn't expecting the question and didn't try to evade it.

— I'm here to see you, Granny—he said.

It was that moment where dying was acknowledged for the first time. Nothing was said. We all knew why we were in the room, that was all. Ma got a bit distressed. With Rossa there she probably knew the end was nearer than she had reckoned. The reality of facing it was beginning to take its toll.

— I need you to get me out of here, Sheila—Ma said.

— I'll talk to the doctors, Ma—Sheila reassured her.

Sheila had a reputation for standing up to the medical profession. She once pulled a drip from her hand in front of a doctor who was condescending towards her. Ma knew that if Sheila couldn't swing it she wasn't coming home. In her heart, she knew her condition was terminal. She had known for longer than she let on in order to try and protect us. When her last-ditch attempt failed, she resigned herself to her fate like the warrior she was.

The fact was that she had a growth on her liver and it was at an advanced stage. She had secondary tumors on her lungs, too. It explained the back pain, and the specialist couldn't, in his heart, advise surgery. It was quite probable that if she went under an anesthetic she would not come out of it. In his opinion, we should accept the situation and let the end be as peaceful as possible. So we did. Ma remained conscious for a few days, and as the pain increased, so did the morphine. Every minute seemed like an hour, and every hour seemed like a day. Ma turning over in the bed became a big event, and when she woke up from a nap it became a cause of celebration. We went through the trauma that all families go through at this time, wanting the best for Ma and above all not wanting her to suffer, not for a minute, not for a second even, no pain for this warrior who had borne pain from the moment of her birth. We wanted no unnecessary suffering at the end, we wanted to give her what she'd always craved, we wanted peace for her, we wanted her free of pain until the last moment and beyond it, when she would, at last, be at peace.

We kept a twenty-four-hour vigil, taking turns to sleep with her in the room. It was strange to lie there in the dead of night and listen to her breathe. Air was her element, as water was Da's. Her energy came from her breath, her passion came up from her lungs and expressed itself through her words. Her breathing marked the time—long, slow, difficult breaths. Sometimes she had to gulp for air, and the fear was she wouldn't get it down, because the morphine made her lethargic. As long as she wasn't distressed, that was the main thing. We were distressed, each one of us getting to spend these last, difficult hours with her, counting her breaths. Yes, we were distressed, and it was perfectly fine, because Ma was not in pain.

At four o'clock in the morning, I woke from a half-sleep. I went over to the bed and she was smiling up at me like a little child.

— Pete, did you get the sports headlines?—she said.

It took me a moment to shake off the sleep. I thought she was rambling.

— Do you need a nurse, Ma?—I asked her.

— No, the racing results, did you get them?—she said.

— No, Ma, I didn't—I said.

— You don't know how Eddery did so?—she said.

Pat Eddery was Ma's favorite jockey. She always included him in her bets with the bookies. As with everything else in her life, she was passionate about her jockeys, her trainers, and her horses. Pat Eddery had done her a favor once (she'd backed four of his mounts and he'd won on them all), and she'd never forgotten him. I had no racing news to give her, and she seemed disappointed. The only thing I could remember was that Roy Keane was out of the Manchester United team for the European Cup Final. He'd accumulated too many yellow cards and wouldn't play. I gave her the news.

— Serves him right, he's a hothead—Ma said.

— He's Irish, Ma, one of our own—I said.

— I don't like Manchester United, they're never happy unless they win—she said.

It was the last conversation I had with her. The following Sunday, at her request, Father Frank Duggan celebrated mass in her room at the Blackrock Clinic. For the previous two days, she'd been in and out of consciousness, and we weren't sure if she'd hold on or not. Sunday arrived, and we crowded into the room—children and grandchildren— and we celebrated a mass that was a celebration of Anna.

Father Frank talked about her going home to her mother, to Peter, and to Frankie, while we secretly hoped for a miracle that might give her a reprieve. He talked about the miracle of life while we prayed for death to stay away. He bowed his head and consecrated the bread and wine. In the silence, Ma drew a large breath and held on to it. She held it for a long, long time, and then slowly she let it go and her head dropped. The struggle was finally over. Shea reached out and took her hand in his. We all followed, laying our hands on her, offering her a sign of peace. Through our bodies, her spirit left the room. It was a beautiful mass, the only beautiful mass I've ever been at. We were holding on to her, her homeless children, and she was gone home. We let go of Ma and hugged each other in our sorrow. What else could we do? We had to look after each other now that she was gone.

We waked her in Stafford's Funeral Home, just as we'd done with Da. We sat in a big circle around her coffin and remembered her life with stories, songs, and anecdotes. Ita recalled the day she killed the rat with a single blow of a brush in the back yard of Seville Place, while Da hid in the house, terrified out of his skin. Johnny gave us a rendition of "Raglan Road," the song by the only poet she ever knew, Paddy Kavanagh from Iniskeen. I told of how I'd caught her smoking in the sitting room and how she'd denied it to my face, while the smoke signals wafted to the ceiling behind her back. As I finished the story, Paul told us there was a good chance she'd be put out of the funeral home during the night. We were all baffled by this, but he assured us it was a strong possibility.

— You know what Ma's like—Paul said.

With that he pointed to a sign on the wall that read NO SMOKING.

— I wouldn't put it past her—he said with a straight face.

The room exploded. We laughed until I thought Ma would get up out of her coffin and tell us to stop. The last time we'd had a wake, Ma had been the master of ceremonies. Now it was her turn to be remembered. Two weeks earlier, we'd celebrated her birthday with her. She'd worn her best suit that day, and she was wearing it again now.

As we sat around the coffin, I couldn't help but think she was pulling a pint for Da in heaven. Or maybe he was pulling one for her. One way or another they were united, just as they'd been in those last years together after their strokes. I couldn't help but think of Doris, too, and how angry she would be when she got the news that Anna had beaten her to it once again.

In the cemetery, we paid the gravediggers to stay away while we took turns shoveling clay on top of Ma's coffin, just as we'd done with Da. After the funeral, we repaired to St. Vincent's GAA Club for tea and sandwiches and hot food. Around eight o'clock, when there was nothing left to say or do, we parted company and went our separate ways. At home, I sat and looked at a blank television screen and wondered how United were getting on in the European Cup Final. One part of me wanted to switch it on, but it was contrary to good manners and funeral customs. Apart from anything else, it would bring bad luck to the team. I had no option but to leave it off. I could never have it on my conscience that I caused United to lose the European Cup. So I said a little prayer and went out to the back garden to kill the time.

I drank four cups of coffee to calm my nerves, but it had the opposite effect. I tried to imagine how the game was going. I had United a goal up at halftime. It was a solo dribble by Dwight Yorke and a side foot into the left-hand corner. I could see the big broad smile, and his teammates trying to catch him for the celebration. Five minutes into the second half, we were two up thanks to a Paul Scholes header. It didn't matter what I dreamt up, the real story was unfolding in Barcelona, and it was on the television, and nothing I could do would change that.

There were five minutes to go, and I couldn't take it any more. I broke with all tradition and pressed the on button. The picture seemed to take forever to materialize. When it did, my heart sank. Bayern Munich of Germany were a goal up. If ever United needed a warrior it was now. There was no Roy Keane. The only warrior I could think of was Ma. She'd prefer to see them lose. Then again, maybe she'd stopped hating them when she'd crossed over into the next life. I had to admit it was highly unlikely. What was I to do? There was a minute left in the game.

I need your help, Ma. United are in big trouble. I'll never ask for another thing as long as I live. Please, get us out of trouble. I know you can do it and if you are going to do it, for God's sake do it now!

As I finished my prayer, United got possession and went up the field. The ball broke loose and came to Teddy Sheringham. He drove the ball along the ground and it hit the back of the net. United were level. Everybody started jumping up and down and hugging each other, but I didn't get excited, not in my normal way. Fiachra and Doireann thought there was something wrong with me. Nuala and Rossa had never seen me so calm at such an exciting time.

— Are you not happy, Da?—they asked me.

— We're going to score again—I said.

I knew Ma was listening. I knew what she was going to do. We won a corner and when the ball was kicked into the box, the inevitable happened. The ball came to Ole Gunnar Solskjaer and he scored. United had won the European Cup and were bringing the trophy back to Manchester. I was excited, of course, but in a quiet way, because of the circumstances. The children couldn't understand how I knew what was going to happen. I told them the result was an answer to a very special prayer. The television commentators said it was a fairytale, but that wasn't true. It was a dispensation granted in heaven, ordained by God in favor of Anna Sheridan, in recognition of the day her body was buried on earth and her spirit went home to be reunited with Peter. It was a victory in heaven that found an echo here on earth.